FAVORITE RAG RUGS

favorite RAG RUGS

Tina Ignell

45 Inspiring Weave Designs

Trafalgar Square Books
North Pomfret, Vermont

First published in the United States of America
in 2007 by Trafalgar Square Books
North Pomfret, Vermont 05053

Printed in China

ISBN: 978-1-57076-370-0

Library of Congress Catalog Control Number: 2006911243

© 2006: Tina Ignell, Bengt Arne Ignell and ICA bokförlag
Forma Publishing Group AB, Västerås

First published in 2006 by
ICA bokförlag
721 85 Västerås
Sweden
www.formapg.se/bok

Reproduction of the contents of this book, in whole or part, is forbidden by copyright law without the express permission of the publisher. This applies to any form of reproduction by printing, copying, taping, electronic storage and dissemination etc.

Forma Publishing Group AB has ISO 14001 environmental certification.

TEXT: Tina Ignell
PHOTOGRAPHY: Bengt Arne Ignell
ENGLISH TRANSLATION: Catherine Zienko
EDITOR: Gunilla Wagner
COVER & DESIGN: Alexandra Frank
ILLUSTRATION: p. 126 Linda Andersson
10 9 8 7 6 5 4 3 2 1

Contents

FOREWORD 7

STRIPES & CHECKS 9
Classic stripes 10
Sunnyside check 12
Strand summer rug 14
Check or stripe 17
Spiral staircase rug 19
Golden straw, golden warp 22
One cloth – one rug 24

STRIPS, CHENILLE & RYA 27
Confetti 28
Dream of Elin 31
Checked by nature 33
Rosette cushion 36
Lambskin puffballs 38
Mosaic 41
Crottle 43
Mocha rya rug 46
Krux 48
Spotty bedside rug 50

CRAMMED & SPACED REPP 53
Day and night 55
A night in June 57
Ladäng rug 60
Blue-white repp stripe 62
Fields of corn 65
Spaced repp jute rug 67
Blue repp lineplay 70

ROSEPATH, DIAMOND TWILL & DRÄLL 73
Rosepath I 75
Rosepath II 77
Rosepath III 80
Half dräll rag rug 82
Diamond twill rag rug 84
Crackle weave rug 87
Rosepath and twill rug 89
Lapping waves on Vättern 92
Watery Reflections 94

TWISTED, THROWN & PATTERNED 97
Meet and part 98
Robust sisal rug in dice weave 100
On the floor, over the table, up the wall 102
Blue bows of sisal 104
Criss-cross inlaid tabby rug 107
Granite 110
Puzzle pieces 112

FIVE RUGS ON ONE WARP 115
Siljan 116
Stranded yarn linen rug 118
Sighing in the rushes 120
Relief 122
Twinkle twinkle lambskin stars 124

Woven edge finish 126
Inspiration 127
Suppliers 128

Foreword

Cutting up worn jeans, old sheeting or a favorite summer frock has more to it than meets the eye. There are memories there. And before that rug gets woven, dreams have been dreamt. Balls of hand cut or sliced rags lie waiting. Arranging a stripe sequence is like composing some music. What tempo shall these stripes have? Fast, slow, erratic. And how do the fabrics look in the weave? A checked fabric in the "Strand summer" rug produced a lovely effect, the big patterned bedspread in the "Check or stripe rug" made a fascinating moire pattern. More often than not you just can't imagine how things will look before that moment when the weft gets beaten in.

"Favorite Rag Rugs" is intended as an ideas bank of patterns and techniques. From one and the same warp you too, as shown in the book, can create essentially different rugs. Starting with a cotton or linen rug warp, you can throw in rags for traditional, striped rugs or weave a golden rug with a weft of glistening rye straw. A linen warp entered for diamond twill can produce a sturdy rug with an intriguing design.

Techniques such as rag inlay and knotted rya bring playfulness and freedom to a weave. Rag inlay, small snippets laid in under a couple of warp ends, could come from fine patterned fabrics or even a bit of lambskin to tickle the feet. Rya knots were bunched into tufty spots on the little bedside rug and an old leather coat was transformed into a round Mocha rya. Infinite potential!

All the rugs in the book come with drafts and detailed directions for warp and weft. Suggestions for finishes are also included with each rug. The rest is over to you! Just as warps can be diverse in color and weft materials varied, one type of finish for a rug might suit the next. Gullvi Heed's rugs feature some beautiful basic finishes and there are directions for making a plied fringe in Stina Larsson's "One cloth – one rug". Go for the finish you think works best. The finish can be what clinches it for the rug.

Weaving rag rugs has enthralled weavers for over a century. Once worn and used fabrics were no longer required in the paper industry, they became the materials that in the majority of homes told the stories of tenderness and care for some of our most personal possessions – our clothes. Some twenty weavers wove and designed the rugs for "Favorite Rag Rugs". All of them have great skill, plenty of imagination and enormous love of weaving. Thanks to them, the book has a wealth of varied material and many highly personalized rugs.

Tina Ignell

Stripes & Checks

Simple stripes and checks constitute an ever expanding universe of pattern. Stripes of plain rag often gain by being juxtaposed with striped, checked or floral fabrics.

Combining rags with other wefts such as straw works beautifully as well. This section also includes directions for an angled rug to go up a spiral staircase.

Classic stripes

DESIGN AND EXECUTION: BRITTA JOHANSSON

Classic striped rag rugs based on the narrow-wide repeat. The color intensity and hue of the rags determine the rest. These rags are from textiles with a past: worn, used and loved.

TECHNIQUE
Tabby, using 4 shafts and 2 pedals

WARP	12/6 unbleached or dyed rug warp yarn, 2 800 m/kg, Blomqvist/Nordiska Textil-Garner
WEFT	1–1.5 cm wide rag strips, taken from old clothes and sheeting woven in cotton
REED	30/10, 1–1 (denotes one end to a heddle and one end to a dent)
SETT	3 ends/cm
SELVAGE	2 ends to a heddle and dent twice on either side
WIDTH IN REED	61 cm
FINISHED WIDTH	56 cm
WEFT SETT	20–23 picks/10 cm
NR. OF ENDS	188
WARP REQUIRED	per meter: 70 g
WEFT REQUIRED	per square meter: 1.2 kg

RUG WITH NARROW STRIPES
Before weaving starts, select and evenly divide up the cut rags for the rug. That way you can create your own stripe sequence and see there are enough rags.

HEM: 4 picks single-stranded rug warp yarn, 11 cm single rags (= first stripe on the rug, plain or patterned, the same type of rag throughout the stripe).

Then weave the repeats with double rags for the length required: 2 plain colored picks, 5.5 cm plain or patterned rags (NB! Use the same rags throughout the stripe). Finish with 11 cm single rags and 4 picks of single-stranded rug warp yarn.

FINISHING
Trim the warp ends ca 15 cm away from the fell at either end. Retain the 4 picks of rug warp yarn. Tie the warp ends off in reef knots, 4 ends to each knot, right the way along the width. Trim the warp ends ca 3 cm from the knots.

Turn the hems under twice, tucking the knots in, and hem with doubled rug warp yarn.

Stitch up the short sides of the hems as well. Hem with the yarn loose enough that the rug does not pull in.

Sunnyside check

DESIGN AND EXECUTION: KERSTIN DANIELSSON

Primarily sunny yellow rags. Closely sett grey warp ends and slender picks of grey create the harmonious check design on this rug.

TECHNIQUE
Tabby, using 2 shafts and 2 pedals

WARP	12/6 unbleached cotton rug warp yarn, 3 120 m/kg
	Grey 12/6 cotton rug warp yarn col.nr. 43, 2 950 m/kg, Bockens yarns, Holma-Helsinglands
WEFT	1.8-2 cm wide washed cotton rags
REED	25/10, unbleached rug warp 1–1; grey rug warp 2–2
SETT	Unbleached = 2.5 ends/cm; grey = 5 ends/cm
SELVAGE	2 ends to a heddle and dent twice on either side
WIDTH IN REED	68 cm
FINISHED WIDTH	63 cm
WEFT SETT	21–22 picks doubled rags/10 cm
NR. OF ENDS	164 ends unbleached rug warp 18 ends dyed rug warp = 182
WARP REQUIRED	per meter: 55 g unbleached rug warp yarn, 7 g dyed rug warp yarn
WEFT REQUIRED	per meter: ca 1 kg

WEAVING
Cut and stitch the ends of the rags together. First weave 4 picks in old rag strips, into which the stretcher can be secured, then ca 1 cm in the unbleached rug warp.

Weave checks for the length required. The checks are woven a little longer than they are wide. To regulate the size of check, use a length of card to measure off the woven length.

When weaving the grey stripe to demarcate the checks, measure off a strip the right length. Place it into the first shed so that equal amounts hang to either side and then insert these to overlap in the next shed. That way you avoid making fastenings on the sides with the grey weft.

FINISHING
Keep 4 picks of the heading (remove the rest). For every 4 ends of the rug, tie 2 extra ends double the length of the fringe ends. Taking 8 ends in each hand, twist both bundles to the right. Then start laying the right bundle over the left until the fringe cord is the length desired. Take one of the ends and twist it twice around the end of the cord, and then make 2 half hitches over the same spot. Trim the fringe evenly with the aid of a cardboard template.

WARP
// = 2 ENDS UNBLEACHED RUG WARP YARN TO A HEDDLE AND DENT
■ = 1 END UNBLEACHED RUG WARP YARN TO A HEDDLE AND DENT
X = 2 ENDS GREY RUG WARP YARN TO A HEDDLE AND DENT

WARP SEQUENCE

UNBLEACHED	42		40		40		42	=164 ENDS
GREY		6		6		6		= 18 ENDS
								=182 ENDS

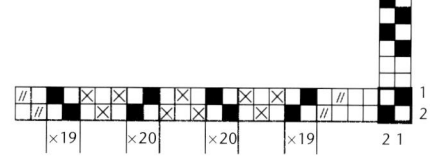

Strand summer rug

REWORKING FROM THE ORIGINAL: TINA IGNELL

This summery rug is at Ellen Keys' Strand by Vättern. The stripes mostly consist of two picks. A stripe of checked rags will nestle up to enhance a plain color. This is a simple way to create a rhythmic repeat.

TECHNIQUE
Tabby, using 4 shafts and 2 pedals

WARP	12/6 unbleached cotton rug warp yarn, 2 800 m/kg, Blomqvist/Nordiska Textil-Garner
WEFT	1–1.5 cm wide rag strips from old clothes and sheeting. Effect stripes: checked rags, ca 1 cm wide
REED	30/10, 1–1
SETT	3 ends/cm
SELVAGE	2 ends to a heddle and dent twice on either side
WIDTH IN REED	ca 61 cm
FINISHED WIDTH	ca 56 cm
WEFT SETT	18–20 picks/10 cm
NR. OF ENDS	188
WARP REQUIRED	per meter: ca 70 g
WEFT REQUIRED	per square meter: ca 1 kg

WEAVING
Weave 1 cm in the cotton rug warp yarn for a heading. Then weave the light rag wefts broken up regularly with blue stripes, as illustrated. Several stripes consist of rags from checked fabrics which are placed to either side of a plain colored weft. Positioning dark checks of a checked fabric over the light checks produces a checked effect in the stripe.

To weave stripes comprising only two picks, use the following method to avoid finishing off on the sides: insert the center part of the requisite length of rag in the first shed and overlap the two tails in the middle of the next shed.

FINISHING
Remove all of the heading except for 4 picks. Tie off 4 ends at a time into overhand knots. Trim the fringes ca 10 cm from the knots.

Check or stripe

DESIGN AND EXECUTION: ANNA SVENSTEDT

An old worn checked bedspread in grey and yellow became the basis of a new rug. The checked patterning gave a fine moiré effect. Closer sett stripes of yellow and green combined with a contrast line of weft produces a checked rug. Just weaving the one color will make the rug lengthways striped.

TECHNIQUE
Tabby, using 2 shafts and 2 pedals

WARP	12/6 grey cotton rug warp yarn, col.nr. 1269, 2 850 m/kg, Borgs Vävgarner Stripes: green col.nr. 37 and yellow col.nr. 15, 2 950 m/kg, Bockens yarns, Holma-Helsinglands
WEFT	ca 1.5 cm single strips of washed strong cotton rags
REED	30/10, grey rug warp 1–1; green and yellow rug warp 1–3
SETT	Grey rug warp = 3 ends/cm; green and yellow rug warp = 9 ends/cm
WIDTH IN REED	74.5 cm
FINISHED WIDTH	72 cm
WEFT SETT	20 picks/10 cm
NR. OF ENDS	259
WARP REQUIRED	per meter: 72 g grey rug warp, 6 g yellow rug warp, 13 g green rug warp yarn
WEFT REQUIRED	per meter: ca 1 kg rags

WEAVING
Weave a hem of about 7 cm in finer rags. Then follow the weft sequence on page 18. Finish with 7 cm for the hem.

FINISHING
Tie off 4 warp ends at a time in overhand knots. Trim leaving about 1 cm of warp end. Turn the hems twice, tuck the knots under and stitch the hem using the rug warp yarn doubled. One stitch into the hem, one stitch into the rug.
(*cont. page 18*)

WARP SEQUENCE

GREEN RUG WARP	9			9		9			9	=36 ENDS
GREY RUG WARP		41		41		41		41		41	=205 ENDS
YELLOW RUG WARP			9					9			=18 ENDS

=259 ENDS

WEFT SEQUENCE

7 cm – hem
15 cm – yellow rags ⎫
2 picks – green stripe
15 cm – grey rags
2 picks – orange stripe
15 cm – yellow rags
2 picks – green stripe
15 cm – yellow rags
2 picks – orange stripe
15 cm – grey rags
2 picks – green stripe
15 cm – yellow rags
2 picks – orange stripe ⎭

Repeat and finish with a yellow check, a grey check and yellow check separated by the narrow stripe + 7 cm hem in fine rags.

WEFT
X = HEM IN FINE GREEN RAGS
■ = FOLLOW THE WEFT SEQUENCE

WARP
X = 1 END GREEN
■ = 1 END GREY
O = 1 END YELLOW

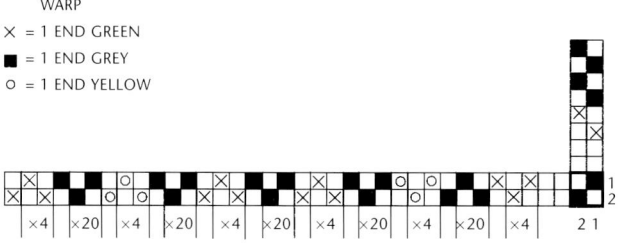

Spiral staircase rug

REWORKING AND WEAVING: TINA IGNELL

A few of these types of rug can be found preserved from the past. Including at Monica Schönberg's in Stockholm. But how were they woven? After a bit of investigation and experimenting we decided to try out using a warp tensioned with weights and fastening the rug with clamps at the breast bar. Maybe the old rugs were made some other way. This way, though, proved to work very well.

TECHNIQUE
Tabby, using 4 shafts and 2 pedals

WARP	12/6 cotton rug warp yarn, black col.nr. 1267, 2 850 m/kg, Borgs Vävgarner
WEFT	ca 2 cm wide cut rags, single strips
REED	30/10, 1–1
SETT	3 ends/cm
SELVAGE	2 ends to a heddle and dent twice on either side
WIDTH IN REED	60 cm
FINISHED WIDTH	ca 58 cm
WEFT SETT	25–28 picks/10 cm
NR. OF ENDS	182
WARP REQUIRED	per meter: 64 g
WEFT REQUIRED	per square meter: ca 1.2 kg

PATTERN DESIGN
First establish the rug's weaving width. Then measure the dimensions of each tread to where it meets the perpendicular rise of the next step.

Draw out a pattern showing each tread and rise. Check the pattern fits by placing it in situ on the stairs. Then use the dimensions of the pattern while weaving. You could also secure the pattern under the weave or cut out the stair treads as pattern pieces and use them as templates. Always make measurements on an untensioned warp.

WARPING
As the outer and inner measurements are to differ on this warp, several warp sections of different lengths can be used. Take measurements at several points on your pattern and divide the warp lengths accordingly. Add 20% for take-up + 50 cm for the weights and 50 cm for thrums. Take care to tie the warp ends tight in the warping so that the ends stay put when being entered and sleyed.

ENTERING, SLEYING AND TIE-ON
The rug warp will not be beamed onto the warp beam but hang weighted behind the back bar. For entering and sleying the warp can be simply tied fast to the back bar. Do the first tie-on while the warp is secured to the back bar. Then suspend 3-5 weights of 1.5 kg each from the warp behind the back bar. Do a second tie-on and check that all the ends are taut. (*cont. page 20*)

WEAVING

Weave ca 1 cm for a heading. Then use finer rags for weaving a 6 cm hem. If the stairs are not angled at the beginning, you can weave as normal. Once the wedge shaped treads start, secure a board with clamps to the breast bar. To produce the wedge shapes, weave in rags to fill the space, see the illustrations. When the rug needs turning, loosen up the clamps, pull the weave on a bit and secure the board with the clamps again.

The rug is not rolled onto the cloth beam but simply passes in front of the cloth beam onto the floor. As the rug draws in a bit it is important to slacken the warp between each stair tread and relax it a little. Always measure off on an untensioned warp. Finish with a 6 cm hem of finer rags.

FINISHING

Tie off 4 ends at a time in overhand knots. Trim 1 cm from the edge. Tuck the fringes into the hems and stitch a 3 cm wide hem open at the sides for the first metal rod.

1. Divide the warp and suspend weights of ca 1.5 kg each from each section.

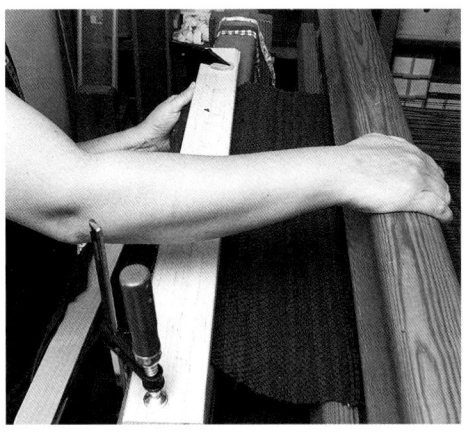

2. The vertical rises between the stair treads are woven straight.

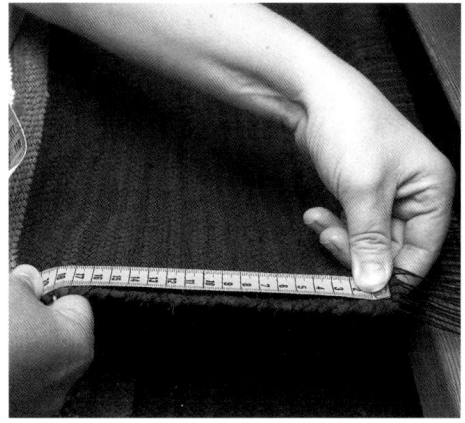

3. Always take measurements on an untentioned warp.

4. Follow the angle of the stair tread by weaving in picks of different lengths. Measure it or use a template of the tread to get the correct angle.

5. The rug is secured at the breast bar with a board and clamps while weaving the angled sections.

6. The batten can be angled to a degree when beating. Lastly, lay the weights on a chair to slacken the warp.

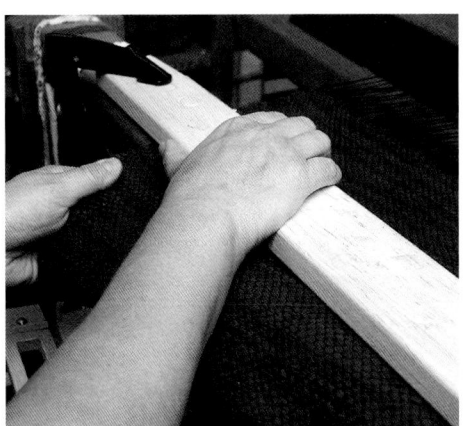

7. Loosen the clamps and pull the rug so that it lines up with the breast bar. Half the angled section is woven on each side of the stripe.

8. The whole stripe is woven the full width of the rug.

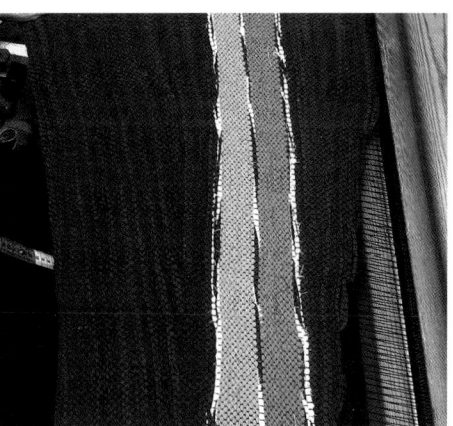

9. The second angled half on the other side of the stripe is woven like the first half. Pull the rug forward so it lines up with the breast bar and continue with the next vertical straight section, see picture 2.

Golden straw, golden warp

DESIGN AND EXECUTION: ANNIKA RUDHOLM

Shimmering straw with broad bands of linen. Simplicity itself. Golden linen yarn in the warp. This rug is edged in a coarse white linen, ideally twill woven.

TECHNIQUE
Basket weave, using 4 shafts and 2 pedals

WARP	12/3 golden bleached linen yarn, 2 900 m/kg, Bockens yarns, Holma-Helsinglands
WEFT	Doubled straws of stripped rye + white cut linen rags, ca 2 cm wide
HEM	12/3 golden bleached linen yarn
REED	50/10, 1–1
SETT	5 ends/cm
WIDTH IN REED	60 cm
FINISHED DIMENSIONS	60 cm × 223.5 cm
WEFT SETT	Rye straw, 25 picks/10 cm White linen rags, 2 picks/cm
NR. OF ENDS	300
WARP REQUIRED	per meter: 105 g
WEFT REQUIRED	per meter: ca 500 g rye straw, ca 25 g white linen rags for the stripes + golden bleached 12/3 linen for the hems

WEAVING
Weave ca 2 cm in the 12/3 linen for a hem. Then weave following the weft sequence. Make a point of beating down well so the rug is firm. Straw shrinks when dry. Lay the straws in so the thicker ends lie to either side. Finish with a 2 cm hem.

STRIPPING AND WEAVING STRAW
Strip the straw and remove the spike. Use a blunt table knife, paring towards the root end.

The straw is softer and easier to weave if moist. Roll it up in a damp cloth the evening before it is being used, but only as much as is needed for one weaving session. Straw lying damp for a longer period will quickly turn moldy.

FINISHING
Tie off the warp ends in twos. Zig-zag the hems, turning them to the reverse of the rug. Fix a robust linen fabric, preferably twill woven, by hand along the long and short sides. This edging is ca 5 cm wide on all sides.

WEFT SEQUENCE
2 cm – 12/3 linen yarn
55 cm – full length doubled rye straws
4.5 cm – white linen rags
50 cm – full length doubled rye straws
4.5 cm – white linen rags
50 cm – full length doubled rye straws
4.5 cm – white linen rags
55 cm – full length doubled rye straws
2 cm – 12/3 linen yarn

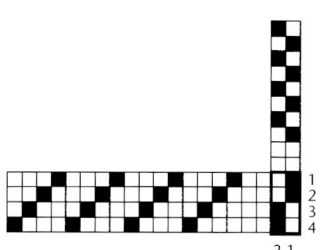

One cloth – one rug

DESIGN AND EXECUTION: STINA LARSSON

Rag rugs are often associated with stripe sequences of different kinds. Yet sometimes you might have an abundant supply of one and the same fabric. The design of the cloth can in itself produce a lovely effect, like this fabric here patterned in turquoise and white.

TECHNIQUE
Tabby, using 4 shafts and 2 pedals

WARP	8/3 unbleached linen warp yarn, 1 700 m/kg, Bockens yarns, Holma-Helsinglands
WEFT	Hand cut or chopped rags, ca 2 cm wide
REED	30/10, 1–1
SETT	3 ends/cm
WIDTH IN REED	68 cm
FINISHED WIDTH	68 cm
WEFT SETT	18–20 picks/10 cm
NR. OF ENDS	204
WARP REQUIRED	per meter: 120 g unbleached linen warp yarn
WEFT REQUIRED	per meter: 800 g cotton rags

WARPING
Divide the number of ends and make the warp in two sections.

WEAVING
Weave eight picks of unbleached 8/3 linen warp yarn for a heading. Arc the weft well. The warp should be kept under a high tension while weaving. Arc the rag weft well. Use a stretcher and move it forward frequently.

FINISHING
Cut down the rug and ply fringes as follows:
   Retain the heading. For each lot of four warp ends, tie in two extra threads twice the length of the fringe ends. Then with four ends in each hand, twist both groups to the right. Keep passing the right bundle over the left until the fringe is the length required and finish with an overhand knot. Trim the fringes even a couple of centimeters from the knots.

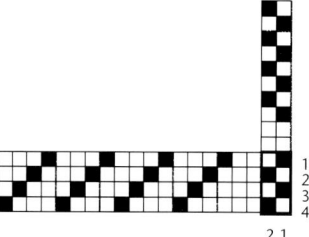

Strips, chenille & rya

Playfulness comes easy in weaves with chenille and little bits of inlay. Inspiration can come from wherever, a rose garden in full splendor or lichen on a slab of stone. Tightly packed fabric inlay, lambskin snippets that puff up into little balls or strips from an old leather coat knotted in a rya. Infinite possibilities.

The chenille rug in this section, Checked by nature, requires some patience. The chenille is woven first, then the rug.

Confetti

DESIGN AND EXECUTION: GULLVI HEED

The blended black ground makes the rag inlay really zingy. To liven up the fields of black, add streaks of dark green, brown and blue rags.

TECHNIQUE
Tabby with rag inlay and pattern weft, using 4 shafts and 3 pedals

WARP	12/6 black cotton rug warp yarn, col.nr. 522, 2 950 m/kg, Bockens yarns, Holma-Helsinglands
WEFT	ca 2 cm wide cut cotton rag strips, + small lengths for the inlay
REED	40/10, 1–1
SETT	4 ends/cm
SELVAGE	2 ends to a heddle and dent twice on either side
WIDTH IN REED	62 cm
FINISHED WIDTH	60 cm
WEFT SETT	25–26 single rag strips/10 cm
NR. OF ENDS	256
WARP REQUIRED	per meter: 86 g
WEFT REQUIRED	per meter: ca 650 g cotton rags

INLAY DESIGN
Weave one pick between each of the inlay picks.

Place the two outermost inlays under 6 raised warp ends, 10 ends in from the selvages. Place two inlays on either side of the rug center, under 6 raised warp ends, separated by 61 ends and ca 61 ends from the two outer inlaid strips.

Then arrange the inlaid wefts over the following picks by moving them 6 ends sideways a total of 7 times before reversing the pattern, see the picture.

WEAVING
Use a stretcher and move it forward frequently. Follow the weft sequence. Take care to arc the rug warp yarn weft well.

FINISHING
Tie off 4 warp ends at a time in overhand knots. Trim the fringes to a suitable length.

WEFT SEQUENCE
12 picks – rug warp yarn
7 cm – black blend
1 pick – yellow
2 picks – grey
1 pick – pattern pedal 3
2 picks – grey
1 pick – yellow
3 picks – black blend
Rag inlay border
3 picks – black blend
1 pick – yellow
2 picks – grey
1 pick – pattern pedal 3
2 picks – grey
1 pick – yellow
34 cm – black blend

Repeat for the length required, finishing with the rag inlay border + 7 cm of the black blend and 12 picks in rug warp yarn.

ANOTHER OPTION IS TO DO A STRAIGHT ENTRY ON FOUR SHAFTS AND INSERT THE PATTERN PICK MANUALLY OVER 4 AND UNDER 4 ENDS ACROSS THE CLOSED SHED.

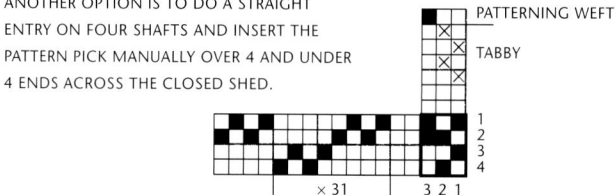

Dream of Elin

DESIGN AND EXECUTION: GULLVI HEED

Small roses of rag inlay packed tight. Stems embroidered in stemstitch. The leaves are inlaid into the same shed as the tabby. This is one way you can decorate a rug with a free design.

TECHNIQUE
Tabby, rag inlay, inlay, twisted weft and embroidery
4 shafts and 2 pedals

WARP	Unbleached 8/3 linen warp yarn, 1 700 m/kg, Bockens yarns, Holma-Helsinglands
WEFT	Cotton rag strips, 1.5–2 cm wide
REED	40/10, 1–1
SETT	4 ends/cm
SELVAGE	2 ends to a heddle and dent twice on either side
WIDTH IN REED	62 cm
FINISHED WIDTH	60 cm
WEFT SETT	25–26 picks/10 cm
NR. OF ENDS	252
YARN REQUIRED	per meter: 150 g
YARN REQUIRED	per meter: ca 600 g cotton rags

WEAVING
Follow the shedding order, see page 32. Use a stretcher and move it forward frequently. When weaving the hem allowance, arc the weft well.

FINISHING
Tie the ends off in twos. Trim 1 cm from the knots, turn the hems twice and stitch down by hand. Embroider the stems in stemstitch with a strong yarn of choice. *(cont. page 32)*

Edge finish

REVERSIBLE RAG INLAY
A simple wide striped rag rug with borders which have an inlaid design of red flowers and green leaves. What makes the rug a bit special is that it is reversible. The rag inlay is laid around the ground weft to bring out the design on both sides. We found this rug in a house in Havstenssund. It was purchased at a flea market nearby. Quite a little rarity in all its simplicity.

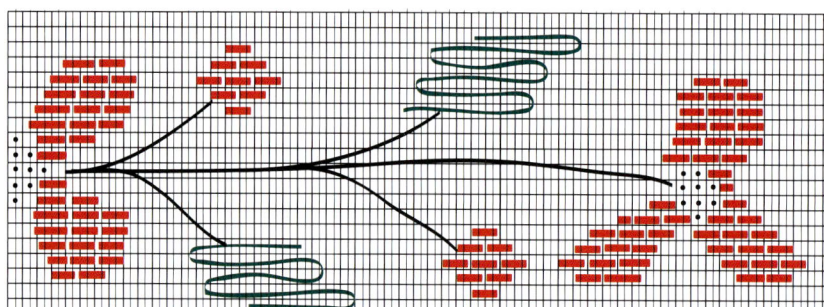

Each vertical column represents one warp end. The inlay is made in an open shed and laid over the rag pick already inserted. Use one strip of rag for one green leaf. For the flowers, cut small strips ca 0.7 cm wide and 2-2.5 cm long.

Try to insert as many rose strips as possible in each shed. Place one strip under two ends and move the motif out by one warp end at a time. Repeat, filling in as many strips as the warp can take before weaving the next pick.

WEFT SEQUENCE FOR THE EDGE
20 picks – 8/3 linen warp yarn
1 pick – grey-blue rug warp yarn ⎫
1 pick – 8/3 linen warp yarn ⎬ × 3
12 picks – 8/3 linen warp yarn
1 pick – grey-blue rug warp yarn ⎫
1 pick – 8/3 linen warp yarn ⎬ × 3
6 picks – 8/3 linen warp yarn

WEFT SEQUENCE FOR THE RUG
15 cm* – mixed blue/brown/grey
9 picks – light rags, well variegated
6 picks – twisted rags **
9 picks – light rags, well variegated
15 cm* – mixed blue/brown/grey
1 pick – pattern weft ***
3 picks – mixed blue/brown/grey
Pattern border as shown in the chart above
4 picks – light rags, well variegated
3 picks – mixed blue/brown/grey
1 pick – pattern weft ***

⎫ Repeat, finishing with 15 cm mixed, border with twisted rag weft, 15 cm mixed + hem allowance

* The block with the basic blue/brown/grey is woven using 3 shuttles alternately. Start with the first rag weft from the right, the second from the left, the third from the right. Do not cut the rags between picks, there will be an attractive little arc over two picks on the sides.

** These rags are cut narrower than the rest and twisted around each other. The first 3 picks slant to the left and the following 3 slant to the right.

*** The pattern weft is passed over 4 then under 4 ends repeatedly across a closed shed.

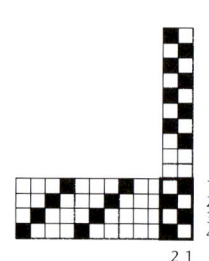

32 ✻ STRIPS, CHENILLE & RYA

Checked by nature

DESIGN AND EXECUTION: GULLVI HEED

Real chenille is quite intriguing while demanding a load of patience. First the chenille strips are woven, lengthways alongside each other, to then form the weft for the weave. With a bit of planning the pattern can be determined beforehand, as here for a checked rug.

Chenille strips

TECHNIQUE
Tabby, using 4 shafts and 2 pedals

WARP	8/2 unbleached cotton yarn, 6 840 m/kg, Bockens yarns, Holma-Helsinglands
WEFT	ca 0.7 cm wide cotton rag strips
REED	80/10, 1 end to a heddle
SLEYING	2 ends to a dent twice, skip 12 ends, etc = 33 times
WIDTH IN REED	57 cm
NR. OF ENDS	132
WARP LENGTH	5.85 m
YARN REQUIRED	113 g 8/2 cotton for a 5.85 m warp

WEAVING
Weave so that loops form on the outermost edges of the weave. These will later be cut open. To weave the checked rug, work as follows:

1. 10 cm light rags across all the groups of ends.
2. 8 cm lilac rags in the 12 right-hand groups of ends, while weaving light rags in the remaining 21 groups of ends.
3. 33 cm light rags.
4. 8 cm green tinged rags in the 12 right-hand groups of ends, while weaving light rags in the remaining 21 groups of ends.
5. 18 cm light rags all the way across all the groups of ends.
6. 8 cm green tinged rags in the 12 right-hand groups of ends, while weaving light rags in the remaining 21 groups of ends.
7. 33 cm light rags across all the groups of ends.
8. 8 cm lilac rags in the 12 right-hand groups of ends, while weaving light rags in the remaining 21 groups of ends.
9. 18 cm light rags across all the groups of ends.

Start again from step 2 and do three repeats in all, finishing with 10 cm light rags instead of 18 cm.

When the weave is finished, snip up the chenille strips through the spaces between the groups of ends. It is easier to do if the cuts are made a bit at a time while unrolling the warp. *(cont. page 34)*

Rug

TECHNIQUE
Tabby, using 4 shafts and 2 pedals

WARP	12/6 unbleached cotton rug warp yarn, 2 800 m/kg, Blomqvist-Nordiska Textil-Garner
WEFT	Chenille + 12/6 rug warp yarn + 8/2 unbleached linen warp yarn
REED	40/10, 1–1
SETT	4 ends/cm
SELVAGE	2 ends to a dent twice on either side
WIDTH IN REED	60 cm
FINISHED DIMENSIONS	60 cm × 110 cm
WEFT SETT	12 chenille picks + 24 rug warp yarn picks/10 cm
NR. OF ENDS	244
WARP REQUIRED	per meter: 88 g unbleached rug warp yarn
WEFT REQUIRED	per rug: handwoven chenille + ca 110 g unbleached rug warp yarn + unbleached 8/2 linen warp yarn for the edges

WEAVING

EDGES: 20 picks in unbleached rug warp yarn. * 1 pick linen warp yarn, 1 pick rug warp yarn, 1 pick linen warp yarn, 3 picks rug warp yarn*. Repeat from *–* 10 times. Finish with 10 picks of the unbleached rug warp yarn. Make sure the weft covers the warp by laying the weft in lots of small arcs.

WEAVING THE RUG: Start by weaving 10 cm in the light chenille, giving it an optional light twist. Weave 2 picks of unbleached rug warp yarn between each chenille pick. Then use the chenille with the check color, laying it in to build up the rug checks. Start with a positioning of 8 cm light, 7 cm lilac, 30 cm light, 7 cm green and 8 cm light. Turn and match up the checks from the other direction.

Each check comprises 12 chenille picks. Weave 10 cm in light chenille only, then weave checks again, placing the green tinged check above the lilac. Make 6 checks and finish with 10 cm light chenille, then the edge.
NB! Don't forget the rug warp yarn picks between each line of chenille.

FINISHING

Tie off 4 warp ends at a time in overhand knots. Trim 1 cm from the knots, fold under and hem the rug with strong thread.

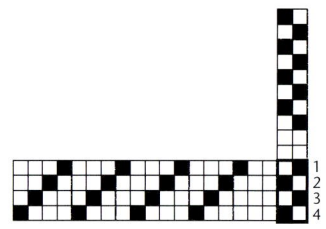

Rosette cushion

DESIGN AND EXECUTION: TINA IGNELL

A fulsome cushion with two different sides. One is covered with inlaid rosettes consisting of really fine rags, several in the same shed. Black linen rags in soumak form the distinctive stripes. The reverse is striped.

TECHNIQUE
Tabby with soumak, using 4 shafts and 2 pedals

WARP	8/2 half bleached linen, 2 420 m/kg, Bockens yarns, Holma-Helsinglands
WEFT	Ground: ca 2 cm wide rag strips cut from sturdy linen
RAG INLAY	Fine fabric strips, 1 cm wide and 5 cm long
REED	40/10, 1–1
SETT	4 ends/cm
SELVAGE	2 ends to a heddle and dent twice on either side
WIDTH IN REED	59.5 cm
FINISHED WIDTH	ca 59 cm
WEFT SETT	25 picks/10 cm
NR. OF ENDS	242
WARP REQUIRED	per meter: 100 g 8/2 linen
WEFT REQUIRED	per meter: ca 800 g linen rags + offcuts of finer fabric for the inlay

WEAVING
Weave 2 cm in the 8/2 linen. Then weave 6 cm tabby in the white linen rags. The stripes are worked as follows: cut a rag strip ca 3 times the width of the weave (stitching strips together if necessary). Lay the rag over two ends, pass back under 1 end, over 2 ends, back under 1 and so on, see the diagram. Weave four picks of white linen rags between each row of soumak. Make 4 soumak stripes. Then weave 4 cm tabby.

Now come the rosettes. Find the mid-point of the weave and mark off by tying a thread in the reed. Measure 7.5 cm to either side of the mid-point and mark off again. These markings will help place the rosettes in line with each other. The inlay is worked as follows: start with the centrally placed rosette. Insert 4-5 fine strips together under 2 raised warp ends. Weave one rag pick. Make the next lot of inlay above the first, but now under 3 raised warp ends. Weave 2 tabby picks. The final inlay for the rosette is under 2 raised ends. Weave 6 cm of tabby. Position the next rosettes where you want them. The reed markings will be useful as a guide for an ordered design.

Once the face has been completed, ca 80 cm, weave 4 picks in 8/2 linen. Weave the reverse with some stripes in the same fabrics as were used for the rosettes. Finish by weaving 2 cm in 8/2 linen.

FINISHING
Tie off the warp ends in 2s. Zig-zag the edges. With right sides facing, stitch up the long sides. Turn inside side out, insert a cushion pad and stitch up the short side. Tug on the inlay gently to form into rosettes.

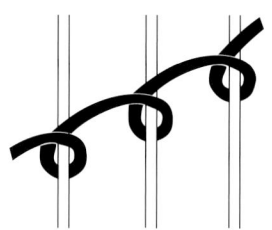 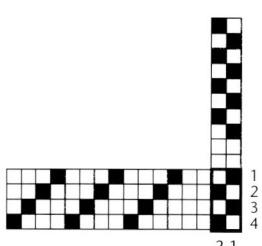

Lambskin puffballs

DESIGN AND EXECUTION: TINA IGNELL

Sheepskin snippets are rewarding to work with. They fluff up into little balls. Soft underfoot.

TECHNIQUE
Tabby with inlay, using 4 shafts and 2 pedals

WARP	8/2 half-bleached linen, 2 420 m/kg, Bockens yarns, Holma-Helsinglands
WEFT	Ground: ca 1.5 cm wide cut rags of fine cotton
	Inlay: snippets cut from a lambskin with fine crimp, ca 0.7 cm wide + heading of 8/2 half-bleached linen
REED	40/10, 1–1
SETT	4 ends/cm
SELVAGE	2 ends to a heddle and dent twice on either side
WIDTH IN REED	59.5 cm
FINISHED WIDTH	ca 59 cm
WEFT SETT	22 picks/10 cm
NR. OF ENDS	242
WARP REQUIRED	per meter: 100 g 8/2 linen
WEFT REQUIRED	per meter: 800 g cut rags and ca 10 × 20 cm lambskin

WEAVING
Weave some picks of 8/2 linen. Then weave 14 cm of tabby before starting on the lambskin snippets inlay. Find the mid-point of the weave and mark off by tying a thread in the reed. Measure 7.5 cm to either side of the mid-point and mark off again. These markings will help line up the inlay.

Work the inlay as follows, starting with the center inlay. Place a snippet under 3 raised warp ends. Pull the fleece up between the ends. Insert the other pieces of inlay 15 cm to either side of the center. Weave two rag picks. Make the next row of inlay above the first but under 5 raised warp ends. Weave two tabby picks. Make the final row of inlay under the same 3 raised ends as for the first row. Weave 12 cm tabby.

The next rows of inlay are woven the same way, but placing the puffballs between those of the first row.

FINISHING
Tie off the warp ends in 2s. Zig-zag the edges. Use some strong fabric in a fitting color and pattern to edge the long and short sides. Sew by hand, making the trim ca 2 cm wide on each side.

Mosaic

DESIGN AND EXECUTION: ANNIKA ANDERSSON

A delicious rug with finely shaded inlaid quadrants. The small pieces of cloth are folded beforehand, hiding the frayed edges at either end, then folded in half lengthways. The closely placed inlay builds up a lovely relief effect and allows for inspiration and play with shifting hues.

TECHNIQUE
Tabby with inlay, using 4 shafts and 2 pedals

WARP	12/6 cotton rug warp yarn, beige col.nr. 44 and black col.nr. 522, ca 2 950 m/kg, Bockens yarns, Holma-Helsinglands
WEFT	Hand-dyed cotton strips, ca 2 cm wide
REED	30/10, beige rug warp 1–1; black stripes 2–2
SETT	Beige rug warp = 3 ends/cm; black stripes = 6 ends/cm
SELVAGE	2 ends to a heddle and dent twice on either side
WIDTH IN REED	143.6 cm
FINISHED DIMENSIONS	138 × 138 cm
WEFT SETT	17 doubled rag picks/10 cm
NR. OF ENDS	441
WARP REQUIRED	per meter: 145 g beige, 5 g black
WEFT REQUIRED	per rug: ca 3 kg cotton rags for the ground + 3 564 strips of inlay

RAG INLAY
The fine strips of inlay are made from pieces ca 5–7 cm long and 1.4 cm wide. To have as little frayed fabric showing as possible, first fold the short sides of each strip to the middle (overlapping by a couple of millimeters). Then fold the strip in half lengthways. The strip is now ca 2–3 cm long and 0.7 cm wide. The inlay is inserted under 2 or 3 raised warp ends on top of the shuttle woven weft. See the diagram on page 42.

WEAVING
Weave a hem of single rag strips, followed by a single black pick as a marker. The ground is woven in doubled rag weft, using two stick-shuttles – one from either side – for neat edges.

Weave the outermost checks as follows: ca 6.5 cm ground, then two quadrants of inlay, one in each corner, outside the black warp ends. See the illustration. The quadrant is built up as shown in the pattern layout overleaf and consists of 59 strips of inlay in total over 17 picks. Ca 6.5 cm ground is woven again, and these outer checks are completed with one black pick.

The central area comprises a total of 64 quadrants, with 52 strips of inlay and 15 picks each. See the illustration and the pattern layout for the placing of the quadrants. Before the first and after the last row of quadrants weave 2 ground picks.

There are 3 ground picks between each row of quadrants. (*cont. page 42*)

QUADRANTS – PATTERN LAYOUT

The figures inside the brackets indicate the number of raised warp ends under which the strip of inlay is placed. The other figures show the number of raised warp ends skipped between the strips of inlay.

```
    (3) 2 (3) 2 (3)        ⎫
(2) 2 (2) 2 (2) 2 (2)      ⎬  Repeat 7 times for the
    (3) 2 (3) 2 (3)        ⎭  central quadrants and
                              8 times for the corner
                              quadrants.
```

CENTRAL AREA – LAYOUT

(x) indicates one quadrant, see the pattern layout above. Figures indicate the number of raised warp ends skipped between quadrants.

```
                    2 PICKS
2 (X) 5 (X) 5 (X) 5 (X) 5 (X) 5 (X) 5 (X) 5 (X) 2
                    3 PICKS
2 (X) 5 (X) 5 (X) 5 (X) 5 (X) 5 (X) 5 (X) 5 (X) 2
                    3 PICKS
2 (X) 5 (X) 5 (X) 5 (X) 5 (X) 5 (X) 5 (X) 5 (X) 2
                    3 PICKS
2 (X) 5 (X) 5 (X) 5 (X) 5 (X) 5 (X) 5 (X) 5 (X) 2
                    3 PICKS
2 (X) 5 (X) 5 (X) 5 (X) 5 (X) 5 (X) 5 (X) 5 (X) 2
                    3 PICKS
2 (X) 5 (X) 5 (X) 5 (X) 5 (X) 5 (X) 5 (X) 5 (X) 2
                    3 PICKS
2 (X) 5 (X) 5 (X) 5 (X) 5 (X) 5 (X) 5 (X) 5 (X) 2
                    3 PICKS
2 (X) 5 (X) 5 (X) 5 (X) 5 (X) 5 (X) 5 (X) 5 (X) 2
                    2 PICKS
```

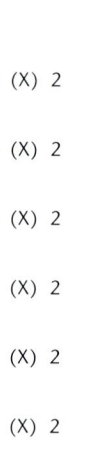

WARP SEQUENCE

BEIGE RUG WARP YARN	72		285		72	=429 ENDS
BLACK RUG WARP YARN		6		6		=12 ENDS

=441 ENDS

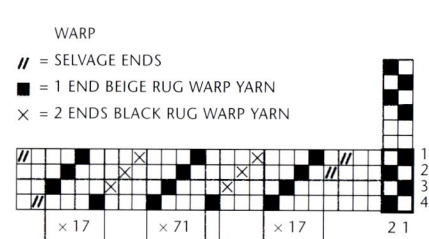

WARP
// = SELVAGE ENDS
■ = 1 END BEIGE RUG WARP YARN
× = 2 ENDS BLACK RUG WARP YARN

Crottle

DESIGN AND EXECUTION: ANNIKA ANDERSSON

Dense rings of fine folded inlay based on the play of color in nature. The rings are positioned slightly differently in their respective checks to tauten the design.

TECHNIQUE
Tabby with inlay, using 4 shafts and 2 pedals

WARP	12/6 cotton rug warp yarn, beige col.nr. 44 and black col.nr. 522, ca 2 950 m/kg, Bockens yarns, Holma-Helsinglands
WEFT	Hand-dyed cotton strips, ca 2 cm wide
REED	30/10, beige warp ends 1–1; black stripes 2–2
SETT	Beige rug warp = 3 ends/cm; black stripes = 6 ends/cm
SELVAGE	2 ends to a heddle and dent twice on either side
WIDTH IN REED	143.6 cm
FINISHED DIMENSIONS	136 × 136 cm
WEFT SETT	16 doubled rag picks/10 cm
NR. OF ENDS	450
WARP REQUIRED	per meter: 145 g beige, 10 g black
WEFT REQUIRED	per rug: ca 3 kg cotton rags

WEAVING
The rug starts with a hem allowance woven in single rags, followed by a single black pick as a marker. The whole rug consists of 36 checks, which are separated by the black warp stripes and single picks of black. Each check contains a ring of inlay strips and each ring has its own distinct positioning both vertically and horizontally to put extra life into the design. To make the ring as round as possible, use a template against the rug. The ground is woven throughout with a weft of doubled rags, using two stick-shuttles – one from either side – for neat edges.

The strips of inlay are made of rags ca 6 cm long and 1.4 cm wide. To have as little frayed fabric showing as possible, first fold the short sides of each strip to the middle (preferably overlapping by a couple of millimeters). Then fold the strip in half lengthways. The strip is now ca 2 cm long and 0.7 cm wide. The inlay is inserted under 2 raised warp ends on top of the shuttle woven weft.

FINISHING
Turn the hems under twice and sew down by hand with rug warp yarn. (*cont. page 44*)

WARP SEQUENCE

BEIGE 12/6 COTTON RUG WARP YARN	72		69		69		69		69		72	=420 ENDS
BLACK 12/6 COTTON RUG WARP YARN		6		6		6		6		6		=30 ENDS

=450 ENDS

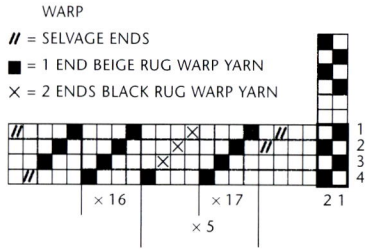

WARP
// = SELVAGE ENDS
■ = 1 END BEIGE RUG WARP YARN
✕ = 2 ENDS BLACK RUG WARP YARN

Mocha rya rug

DESIGN AND EXECUTION: MARIE ROLANDER

Here an old leather coat got cut up into small bits and then used in rya knots on a spectacular round rug. Cut pieces of fabric work just as well as leather offcuts.

TECHNIQUE

Rya on a tabby/hopsack ground, using 4 shafts and 4 pedals

WARP	12/6 cotton rug warp yarn, black col.nr. 1267, 2 850 m/kg, Borgs Vävgarner
WEFT	Ground: jute, black col.nr. 918, ca 600 m/kg. Borgs Vävgarner; Rya knots: ca 8 cm long and 3–5 mm wide leather strips
REED	30/10, 1–1
SETT	3 ends/cm
SELVAGE	2 ends to a heddle and dent twice on either side
WIDTH IN REED	82 cm
FINISHED DIMENSIONS	ca 75 cm diameter
WEFT SETT	ca 7 jute picks/cm
NR. OF ENDS	250
WARP REQUIRED	per meter: ca 90 g
WEFT REQUIRED	per rug: ca 800 g jute, ca 1 kg strips of leather

WEAVING

The rug is woven square on the loom. Draw out a round paper template, ca 70 cm in diameter. Weave 5 cm tabby in the jute. Start with the rya knots in the middle of the rug after weaving a pick of hopsack, see the shedding order. The rya knots are tied over two raised ends, see the diagram.

Tie 5 leather strips in the first row of knots, 16 in the second, 19 in the third, 22 in the fourth etc. Follow the template to keep the rug round.

Finish with 5 cm for the hem allowance.

FINISHING

After cutting down, the circle shape may need adjusting by unpicking some rya knots lying outside the circumference. Then using chalk, mark a circle ca 3 cm beyond the outer knots. Zig-zag over this line a couple of times and glue along it. Let the glue dry and then cut out the circle. Edge with leather, coarse fabric or tape.

The rya knots are tied in these sheds over two raised ends. No ground picks are drawn in.

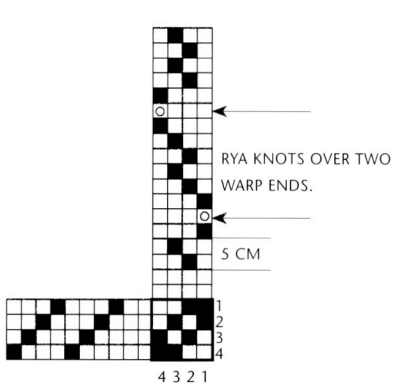

Krux

DESIGN: BARBRO LOMAKKA   WEAVE: SONJA ERIKSSON

A rag inlay rug, but all in wool with vadmal scraps and rya knots placed in a grid design. The weft is rug wool yarn, the warp linen.

TECHNIQUE
Tabby with rag inlay and rya knots, using 4 shafts and 2 pedals

WARP	8/5 unbleached linen warp yarn, 950 m/kg, Bockens yarns, Holma-Helsinglands
WEFT	Hem: Wålstedts gobelin yarn, natural grey, ca 2 500 m/kg Ground: Wålstedts rug wool yarn, doubled, light grey col.nr. 90/10, 850 m/kg
RYA KNOTS	Wålstedts UllMa rya yarn, rust col.nr. 3, 875 m/kg (the length of yarn, unknotted, for a rya knot is ca 7cm)
INLAY	Dark grey vadmal (each segment is 2 × 5 cm)
REED	20/10, 1–1
SETT	2 ends/cm
SELVAGE	2 ends to a heddle and dent twice on either side
WIDTH IN REED	88 cm
FINISHED DIMENSIONS:	ca 86 × 200 cm
WEFT SETT	Hem: see under weaving; Ground: ca 4 doubled picks/cm
NR. OF ENDS	180
WARP REQUIRED	per meter: 190 g
WEFT REQUIRED	per rug: hem, 100 g gobelin yarn; ground, ca 1850 g rug wool yarn; rya knots, ca 100 g; inlay, ca 1 sq. m. vadmal

WEAVING
8.5 cm hem as follows: 2 picks of linen warp yarn, 4 cm of gobelin yarn (ca 10 picks/cm), 4.5 cm in the gobelin yarn, where the weft is laid in generous arcs so that the warp is not visible.
Then weave 2.5 cm in the rug wool yarn doubled.

VADMAL INLAY 1 Start 2.5 cm in from the left outer edge. Lay the vadmal under 2 raised warp ends, skip 5 ends and lay in the next segment under 2 raised ends, repeat across. Altogether there should be 21 inlaid pieces of vadmal. Then weave 3 picks of the doubled rug wool yarn. Tie rya knots over the same warp ends raised for the vadmal inlay, then weave 3 picks of doubled rug wool yarn.

VADMAL INLAY 2 Lay the pieces of vadmal under the same warp ends as for the previous inlay pattern. Then weave 3 picks of doubled rug wool yarn.

VADMAL INLAY 3 Now start on the checked pattern. Inlay a piece of vadmal over every 6th of the vadmal segments, totalling 5 pieces of inlay. These scraps are laid under the same warp ends as before. Then weave 3 picks in the doubled rug wool yarn, rya knots, 3 picks in rug wool yarn etc. Do 13 of these vertical vadmal inlays. From the first of these 13 up to the 13th vadmal inlay the check should measure ca 20 × 20 cm.

The vadmal inlay sequence 1–3 forms one repeat. Weave for the length required. Finish with the inlay sequence 1 and 2 + the hem allowance.

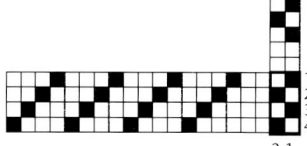

Spotty bedside rug

DESIGN AND EXECUTION: HELENA BENGTSSON

Make rya roundels in strong yarn on a tabby base of strong linen rags.

TECHNIQUE
Tabby and rya knots, using 4 shafts and 2 pedals

WARP	8/4 unbleached linen warp yarn, 1 200 m/kg, Borgs Vävgarner
WEFT	Ground: ca 2 cm cut rags of strong linen
	Rya knots: 3 strands Åsborya, wine red col.nr. 4090, 1 200 m/kg, Borgs Vävgarner
	+ 2 strands Mattlin, green col.nr. 1095, 400 m/kg, Bockens yarns, Holma-Helsinglands
REED	30/10, 1–1
SETT	3 ends/cm
SELVAGE	2 ends to a heddle and dent twice on either side
WIDTH IN REED	54.5 cm
FINISHED WIDTH	ca 54 cm
WEFT SETT	ca 20 picks/10 cm
NR. OF ENDS	168
WARP REQUIRED	per meter: 140 g
WEFT REQUIRED	per meter: 800 g linen rags + yarn for the rya knots

WEAVING
Weave 12 picks of linen warp yarn, followed by 8 picks of white linen rags. Tie a marker thread at five different places on the reed so that the rya knots land up in line with each other: start from the right, tying the first thread 17 dents in from the selvage, with the next three threads at intervals of 33 dents and the final thread on the left tied 16 dents in from the side. The rya knots are tied over 2 ends with no warp ends between the knots, as follows:

RYA KNOTS ROW 1: Tie three rya knots with 3 strands of rya yarn, ca 10 cm long, at each of the places marked off by threads on the reed. Weave one rag pick.

RYA KNOTS ROW 2: Two wine red rya knots, 1 green rya knot in Mattlin, 2 wine red (the green rya knot is tied over the middle knot of row 1).

RYA KNOTS ROW 3: as row 2.

RYA KNOTS ROW 4: as row 1.

Weave ca 15 picks of rag weft before the next row of rya spots. Weave 8 rows of rya spots, finishing with 8 picks of linen rags and 12 picks in the linen warp yarn.

FINISHING
Tie off 6 ends at a time in overhand knots. Trim the fringes even.

CARE
Remove marks with a mild washing agent and an old cloth. When the rya knots are of wool, as in this case, dry-cleaning is recommended for cleaning the whole rug.

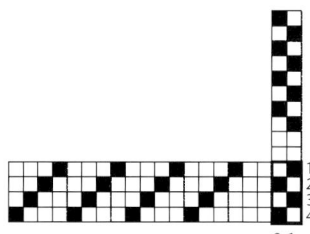

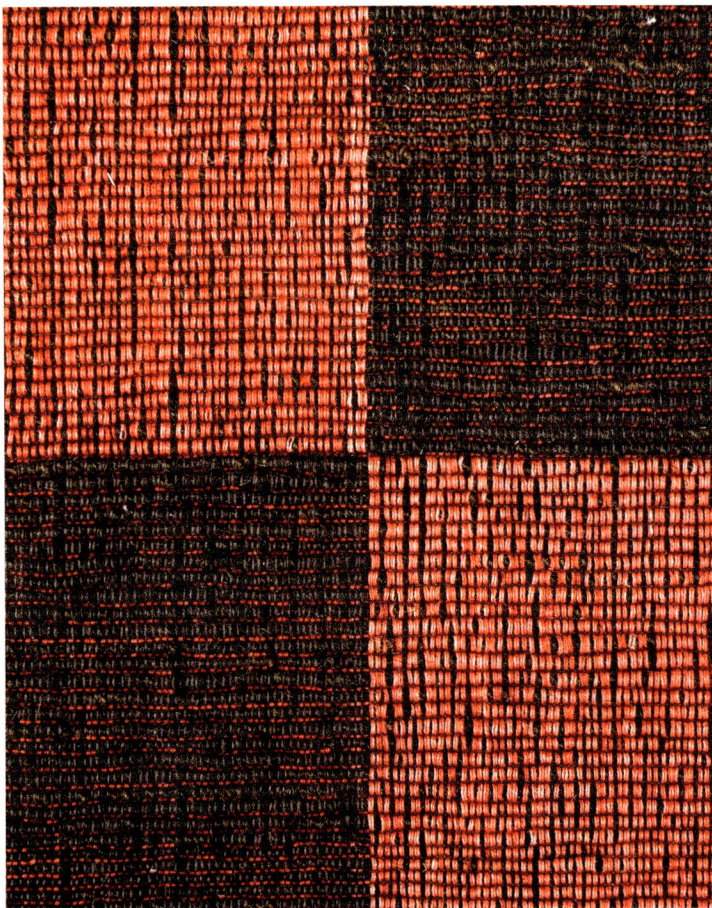

Crammed & spaced repp

Crammed and spaced stripes allow for loads of variation. From the closest sett repp to rugs where lines of weft shine through the spaces of a warp sett at closer and wider intervals.

Top left: Spaced repp jute rug, p 67.
Below left: Ladäng rug, p 60.
Left: A night in June, p 57.

Day and night

REWORKING FROM THE ORIGINAL: TINA IGNELL

An elegant design based on dark and light spaced stripes in the warp. The weft is composed of many different fabrics, light and dark. Start by sorting the rags according to chroma and then work out a stripe sequence. A rose/red stripe punctuates the flow.

TECHNIQUE
Spaced repp, using 4 shafts and 2 pedals

WARP	12/6 cotton rug warp, grey col.nr. 43, light grey col.nr. 42, 2 950 m/kg, Bockens yarns, Holma-Helsinglands
WEFT	1 cm wide rags + 12/6 rug warp yarn, brown col.nr. 61, 2 950 m/kg, Bockens yarns, Holma-Helsinglands
REED	50/10, 1–1
SETT	5 ends/cm
WIDTH IN REED	56 cm
FINISHED WIDTH	52 cm
WEFT SETT	14 single rags + 14 picks rug warp yarn/10 cm
NR. OF ENDS	280
WARP REQUIRED	per meter: 56 g dark grey rug warp yarn, 40 g light grey rug warp yarn
WEFT REQUIRED	per meter: 57 g brown rug warp yarn + ca 600 g single rags

WEAVING
Use a stretcher and move it forward frequently. Weave a 3 cm hem in the brown 12/6 rug warp yarn. Follow the weft sequence.
   Finish with a dark check and 3 cm hem allowance.

FINISHING
Turn the hems under twice and hem with the rug warp yarn. *(cont. page 56)*

WEFT SEQUENCE, 1 REPEAT

3 cm hem – brown rug warp yarn

6 cm – dark rags – Block I	
1 cm – dark rags – Block II	
1 cm – dark rags – Block I	
6 cm – dark rags – Block II	} dark check
1 cm – dark rags – Block I	
1 cm – dark rags – Block II	
6 cm – dark rags – Block I	
1 cm – rose rags – Block II	
1 cm – grey rags – Block I	
1 cm – red rags – Block II	} stripe I
1 cm – grey rags – Block I	
1 cm – rose rags – Block II	
6 cm – light rags – Block I	
1 cm – light rags – Block II	
1 cm – light rags – Block I	
6 cm – light rags – Block II	} light check
1 cm – light rags – Block I	
1 cm – light rags – Block II	
6 cm – light rags – Block I	
1 cm – rose rags – Block II	
1 cm – grey rags – Block I	
1 cm – rose rags – Block II	} stripe II
1 cm – grey rags – Block I	
1 cm – rose rags – Block II	

WARP SEQUENCE

DARK GREY 12/6 RUG WARP YARN	24	116	24	=164 ENDS
LIGHT GREY 12/6 RUG WARP YARN		116		=116 ENDS

=280 ENDS

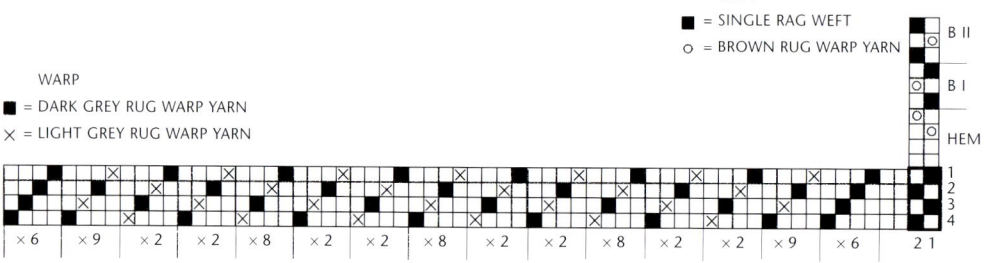

56 ✳ CRAMMED & SPACED REPP

A night in June

DESIGN AND EXECUTION: GULLVI HEED

A gloaming in the midnight blue and red. See the illustrations on pages 53 and 59.

TECHNIQUE
Spaced repp, using 4 shafts and 2 pedals

WARP	12/6 unbleached cotton rug warp yarn, 3 120 m/kg
	Dyed 12/6 cotton rug warp yarn, black col.nr. 522, blue col.nr. 34, red col.nr. 1007, rust col.nr. 36, 2 950 m/kg, Bockens yarns, Holma-Helsinglands
WEFT	Cut cotton rags ca 1.5 cm wide + unbleached 12/6 rug warp yarn and black 12/6 rug warp yarn
REED	40/10, 1–2
SETT	8 ends/cm
WIDTH IN REED	57 cm
FINISHED WIDTH	56.5 cm
WEFT SETT	ca 20 rag picks + 20 rug warp yarn picks/10 cm
NR. OF ENDS	456
WARP REQUIRED	per meter: 43 g black rug warp yarn, 43 g blue rug warp yarn, 45 g unbleached rug warp yarn, 15 g red rug warp yarn, 15 g rust rug warp yarn
WEFT REQUIRED	per meter: ca 550 g cotton rags, 25 g black rug warp yarn, 10 g unbleached rug warp yarn

ENTRY
The black/blue and red/rust warp ends are entered in the sequence they happen to come.

WEAVING
Weave 5 cm in black rug warp yarn, arcing it well. Then follow the weft sequence. Make your rag strips preferably from old cast-off clothes and worn textiles and mix many different shades in the blue area.

FINISHING
Tie off three ends at a time. Trim ca 1 cm from the knots, turn under and hem by hand in strong thread.

WARP SEQUENCE

BLACK + BLUE		8		8		8				8		8			8	8	8	=64
RED + RUST			8														8	=16
2 ENDS UNBLEACHED + BLACK + BLUE					24		24		12		24		112	24		12	24		24		=280
BLACK + BLUE + RED + RUST								24		24					24	24			=96

=456 ENDS

WARP
- ■ = 1 END BLACK OR 1 END BLUE ENTERED IN NO SPECIAL ORDER
- O = 1 END RUST OR 1 END RED ENTERED IN NO SPECIAL ORDER
- X = UNBLEACHED

WEFT
- ■ = BLACK RUG WARP YARN
- X = BLUE COTTON RAGS
- O = BLACK COTTON RAGS
- ╱ = UNBLEACHED COTTON RAGS
- + = UNBLEACHED RUG WARP YARN
- • = RED COTTON RAGS

×2 | ×2 | ×2 | ×6 | ×2 | ×6 | ×6 | ×3 | ×6 | ×6 | ×2 | ×28 | ×2 | ×6 | ×6 | ×3 | ×6 | ×6 | ×2 | ×6 | ×2 | ×2 | ×2 | 2 1

REPEAT ×15

×15
5 CM

CRAMMED & SPACED REPP

Ladäng rug

REWORKING FROM THE ORIGINAL: TINA IGNELL

This checked rug in crammed and spaced repp was woven nearly one hundred years ago by Gerda Ignell of southern Närke. A classy design that holds its own even now. Combining red and rose in the warp will recreate the feel of the older version in the new rug.

TECHNIQUE
Crammed and spaced repp, using 4 shafts and 2 pedals

WARP	16/2 cotton yarn, red col.nr. 117, dark rose col.nr. 259, brown col.nr. 278, 12 800 m/kg, Borgs Vävgarner
WEFT	Thick: rug yarn 1,25 (two strands combined), natural black col.nr. 5013, 1 250 m/kg, Borgs Vävgarner (or 1 cm wide rags in brown or black woollen fabric) Thin: 16/2 cotton, brown col.nr. 278, doubled, Borgs Vävgarner
REED	70/10
ENTRY	red + dark rose 16/2 cotton, 2 ends to a heddle, entered in no special order 16/2 brown cotton, 1 end to a heddle
SLEYING	3 ends to a dent = 2 ends (1 red + 1 dark rose) + 1 brown
SETT	21 ends/cm
WIDTH IN REED	64.3 cm
FINISHED WIDTH	60 cm
WEFT SETT	3 thin and 3 thick picks/cm
NR. OF ENDS	1 350

WARP REQUIRED per meter: 70 g red and rose 16/2 cotton (35 g in each shade) + 35 g brown 16/2 cotton

WEFT REQUIRED per meter: 300 g rug yarn + 31 g brown 16/2 cotton (or 300 g woollen rag strips + 31 g brown 16/2 cotton)

WARP SEQUENCE
Warp up with 3 ends at a time (1 in each shade)

WEAVING
Use a stretcher and move it forward frequently. Weave a 4 cm hem in the brown 16/2 cotton. Follow the shedding order. Finish with a hem allowance again.

FINISHING
Turn the hems under twice and stitch down by hand.

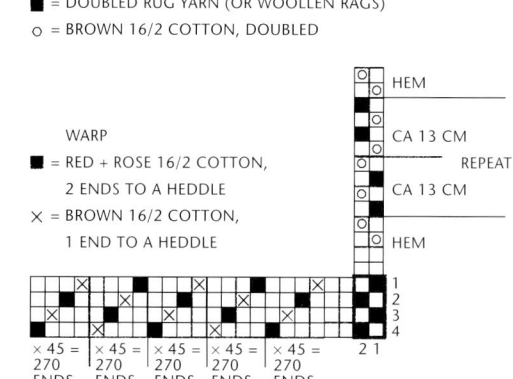

WEFT
■ = DOUBLED RUG YARN (OR WOOLLEN RAGS)
○ = BROWN 16/2 COTTON, DOUBLED

WARP
■ = RED + ROSE 16/2 COTTON, 2 ENDS TO A HEDDLE
× = BROWN 16/2 COTTON, 1 END TO A HEDDLE

Blue-white repp stripe

DESIGN AND EXECUTION: ULLA BERGLUND BRASCH

Classic blue striped repp matting inspired by the striped mats in Carl Larsson's Sundborn. The strong cotton rug warp yarn makes it a pretty quick weave. And the rag weft produces a lovely effect.

TECHNIQUE
Repp, using 4 shafts and 2 pedals

WARP	12/6 cotton rug warp yarn, unbleached, 3 120 m/kg + blue col.nr. 25, 2 950 m/kg, Bockens yarns, Holma-Helsinglands
WEFT	Cut white cotton rags ca 1.5 cm wide
HEMS	Blue cotton rug warp yarn
REED	40/10, 2–4
SETT	16 ends/cm
WIDTH IN REED	60 cm
FINISHED WIDTH	ca 60 cm
WEFT SETT	Hem: ca 5 picks single-stranded rug warp yarn/cm; Mat: 22 picks rags/10 cm
NR. OF ENDS	964
YARN REQUIRED	per meter: 144 g unbleached rug warp yarn, 175 g blue rug warp yarn
YARN REQUIRED	per meter: 600 g

WARPING
Warp up with 2 ends to a portee, length as required. These two ends are doubled in the entry.

WEAVING
A stretcher is not required as the matting does not draw in while being woven. Weave a 7 cm hem in the blue cotton rug warp yarn. Weave the mat proper with single cotton rags. Lay the rag weft in an arc, change shed and beat down several times. Weave for the length required and finish with a 7 cm hem. NB There are no alternating picks of rug warp yarn between each of the rag picks.

FINISHING
Zig-zag carefully along both cut sides on the sewing machine. Turn a 2 cm doubled hem. Using the rug warp yarn, secure the hem in close whipstitch. Use two needles: blue yarn for the blue stripes, unbleached for the unbleached stripes. The thread not in use is tucked into the hem. Both sides turn out as nice as each other making the mat reversible.

WARP SEQUENCE

BLUE RUG WARP YARN	66		64		66	=516 ENDS
UNBLEACHED RUG WARP YARN		64		64		=448 ENDS
		× 6			=964 ENDS

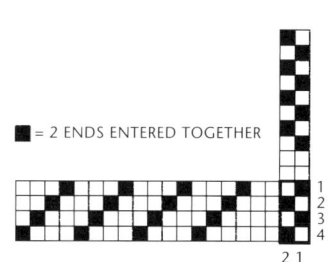

Fields of corn

DESIGN AND EXECUTION: GULLVI HEED

A rug made as a tribute to the rag rugs of yesteryear. Its warp is in various colors and the reed has a higher dentage than those commonly used nowadays. At some points the ends are double-sleyed, which brings out the warp shades. By using rags the same shades as the warp, a checked effect appears. Go for patterned rags in as many different shades as possible, aiming primarily at an overall beige feel.

TECHNIQUE
Tabby and rosepath, using 4 shafts and 6 pedals

WARP	12/6 unbleached cotton rug warp yarn, 3 120 m/kg
	Dyed 12/6 cotton rug warp yarn, yellow col.nr. 15, brown col.nr. 61, 2 950 m/kg, Bockens yarns, Holma-Helsinglands
WEFT	Cut cotton rags ca 1.5 cm wide + linen warp and rug warp yarn for the rosepath edges
REED	50/10, 1 or 2 ends to a dent
SETT	5 ends/cm or 10 ends/cm, see under warp sequence
WIDTH IN REED	61.2 cm
FINISHED WIDTH	59 cm
WEFT SETT	26–27 picks/10 cm
NR. OF ENDS	334
WARP REQUIRED	per meter: 70 g unbleached rug warp yarn, 11 g yellow rug warp yarn, 35 g brown rug warp yarn
WEFT REQUIRED	per meter: ca 700 g cotton rags + 8/2 linen warp yarn and yellow + brown rug warp yarn for the hems

WEAVING
Weave the rosepath edging as given in the weft sequence, see page 66. Tabby doesn't really work for the edge as there are some closer sett stripes in the rug. Make many small arcs of the rug warp weft so that the sides stay put and don't pull in.

Follow the weft sequence for the rug. Arc the rag weft well.

FINISHING
Knot off 3 ends at a time. Trim ca 1 cm from the knots. Stitch some linen fabric or tape against the rosepath edging, fold under and hem in strong thread. The rug is reversible, with different edge finishes showing on either side. (*cont. page 66*)

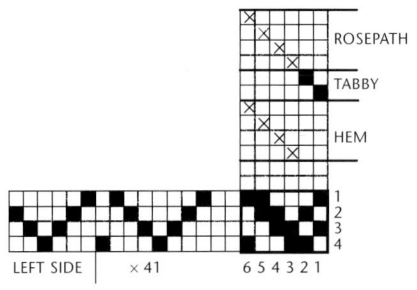

WARP SEQUENCE

UNBLEACHED RUG WARP YARN	④	24	⑧		⑧		⑧		6			6		⑧		⑧		⑧	24	④	=206
YELLOW RUG WARP YARN				8				8			8				8						=32
BROWN RUG WARP YARN						16		16		2			16		16						=96

× 16   =334 ENDS

THE GROUPS OF ENDS MARKED AS NUMBERS IN CIRCLES ARE DOUBLE-SLEYED (TWO ENDS TO A DENT).

WEFT SEQUENCE FOR THE ROSEPATH EDGING WOVEN ON PEDALS 3–6

8 picks – unbleached 8/2 linen warp yarn
4 picks – brown 12/6 rug warp yarn
4 picks – unbleached 8/2 linen warp yarn
4 picks – yellow 12/6 rug warp yarn
4 picks – unbleached 8/2 linen warp yarn
4 picks – brown 12/6 rug warp yarn
4 picks – unbleached 8/2 linen warp yarn
4 picks – yellow 12/6 rug warp yarn
4 picks – unbleached 8/2 linen warp yarn

WEFT SEQUENCE, 1 REPEAT, FOR THE RUG

10 cm – variegated brown/beige rags   } × 2
2 picks – brown rags
10 cm – variegated brown/beige rags
4 picks – yellow rags in rosepath, pedals 3–6
2 picks – unbleached rags
2 cm – brown rags
2 picks – unbleached rags
3.5 cm* – blue rags
2 picks – unbleached rags
2 cm – brown rags
2 picks – unbleached rags
4 picks – yellow rags in rosepath, pedals 3–6

Finish with 10 cm beige rags + 2 picks brown × 2 + 10 cm beige and the hem edging.

* For the second repeat, this stripe is woven in pink, and in green for the third repeat.

Spaced repp jute rug

DESIGN AND EXECUTION: INGRID SKAGERSTRÖM

A checked reversible rug woven with jute weft on a warp of cotton rug warp yarn. An excellent combination, producing both a sturdy rug and a beautiful sheen. On one side the checks are black and beige; on the other there are black, beige and green checks.

TECHNIQUE
Spaced repp, using 4 shafts and 2 pedals

WARP	12/6 cotton rug warp yarn, red col.nr. 1007, beige col.nr. 40, black col.nr. 522, 2 950 m/kg, Bockens yarns, Holma-Helsinglands
WEFT	Thick: doubled Jutegarn, black col.nr. 918, green col.nr. 914, 600 m/kg, Borgs Vävgarner Thin: 12/6 cotton rug warp yarn single-stranded, red col.nr. 1007, Hem: black col.nr. 572, Bockens yarns, Holma-Helsinglands
REED	40/10, 1 or 2 ends to a heddle, 3 ends to a dent
SETT	12 ends/cm
WIDTH IN REED	67 cm
FINISHED WIDTH	67 cm
WEFT SETT	2 thin and 2 thick picks = 1 cm
NR. OF ENDS	804
WARP REQUIRED	per meter: red 50 g, beige 120 g, black 110 g
WEFT REQUIRED	per meter: 50 g red cotton rug warp yarn, 460 g jute (230 g in each shade) + black cotton rug warp yarn for the hems

WARPING
Allow 20% take-up when calculating the warp length. The central section is warped alternating groups of 2 ends beige and 1 end black with groups of 2 ends black and 1 end beige.

WEAVING
First weave 6 cm for the hem in the black cotton rug warp yarn. To keep the weave even, lay the thin cotton rug warp yarn weft in loosely and the doubled jute weft straighter.

FINISHING
Turn under twice to make a 2 cm hem. Stitch down with strong thread, one stitch into the hem and one stitch into the rug. Pull the thread taut as you go. *(cont. page 68)*

WARP SEQUENCE

RED 1007	24			48								48			24	=144 ENDS
BEIGE 40		18			56	28	56	28	56	28	56			18		=344 ENDS
BLACK 522			18		28	56	28	56	28	56	28		18			=316 ENDS
	EDGE 108 ENDS											EDGE 108 ENDS				=804 ENDS

WARP
■■ = RED RUG WARP, 2 ENDS TO A HEDDLE
■ = RED RUG WARP, 1 END TO A HEDDLE
•• = BEIGE RUG WARP, 2 ENDS TO A HEDDLE
• = BEIGE RUG WARP, 1 END TO A HEDDLE
×× = BLACK RUG WARP, 2 ENDS TO A HEDDLE
× = BLACK RUG WARP, 1 END TO A HEDDLE

WEFT
×× = DOUBLED BLACK JUTE
• • = DOUBLED GREEN JUTE
// = RED RUG WARP YARN
■ = BLACK RUG WARP YARN

CHECK 2: ×1, ×12
REPEAT
CHECK 1: ×1, ×12
HEM 6 CM

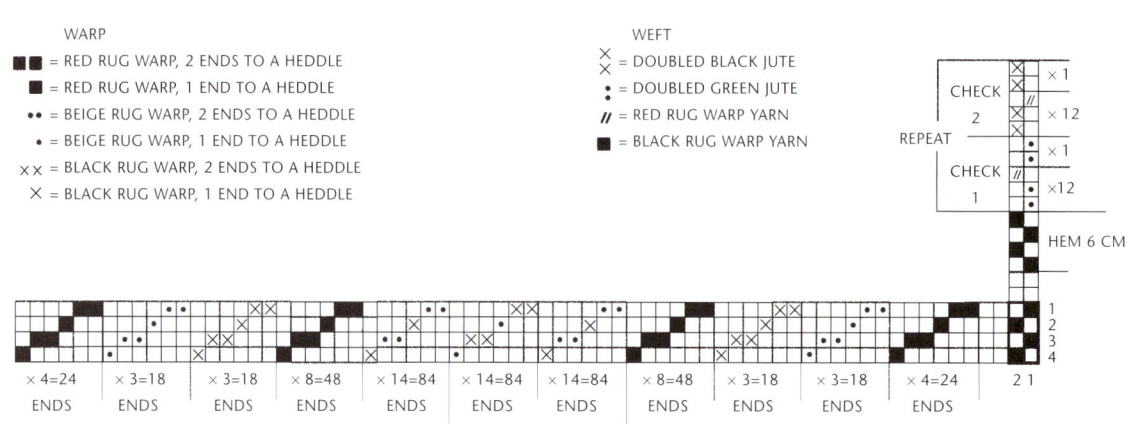

68 ✴ CRAMMED & SPACED REPP

Blue repp lineplay

DESIGN AND EXECUTION: BIRGITTA JOHANSSON

One threading, several shedding orders. These rugs are just two examples of the different types of lineplay that can be woven on this entry. The reverse will have the opposite patterning.

TECHNIQUE
4-block repp, using 10 shafts and 8 pedals

WARP	16/2 cotton, black col.nr. 268, blue col.nr. 258, ca 12 800 m/kg, Borgs Vävgarner
WEFT	Thick: Maxi stranded rug yarn, black col.nr. 5009, 250 m/kg, Borgs Vävgarner
	Thin: 16/2 cotton doubled, black as for the warp
REED	90/10, 2–4
SETT	36 ends/cm
WIDTH IN REED	69.3 cm
FINISHED WIDTH	ca 68 cm
WEFT SETT	17 thick + 17 thin picks/10 cm
NR. OF ENDS	2496
WARP REQUIRED	per meter: 100 g in each shade
WEFT REQUIRED	per meter: 475 g stranded rug yarn, ca 20 g 16/2 cotton

WARPING AND THREADING
Warp up with 4 ends, 2 in each shade. Make three warp chains for more manageable beaming. The rug has four blocks, but the central block is entered on 4 shafts, because otherwise the pedals are quite hard to push down and the ends tend to snag on each other.

WEAVING
Weave the hem allowance in doubled 16/2 cotton for 8 cm. Follow the shedding order for the rug you want to weave.

FINISHING
Turn the hems twice and hand-stitch down in close stitches. The rug is reversible.

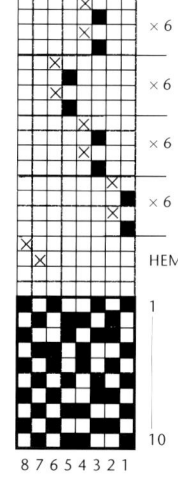

SHEDDING ORDER FOR THE RUG ON THE LEFT

WEFT
■ = THICK WEFT
× = THIN WEFT

SHEDDING ORDER FOR THE RUG ON THE RIGHT

WARP
○ = 2 ENDS BLUE 16/2 COTTON
■ = 2 ENDS BLACK 16/2 COTTON

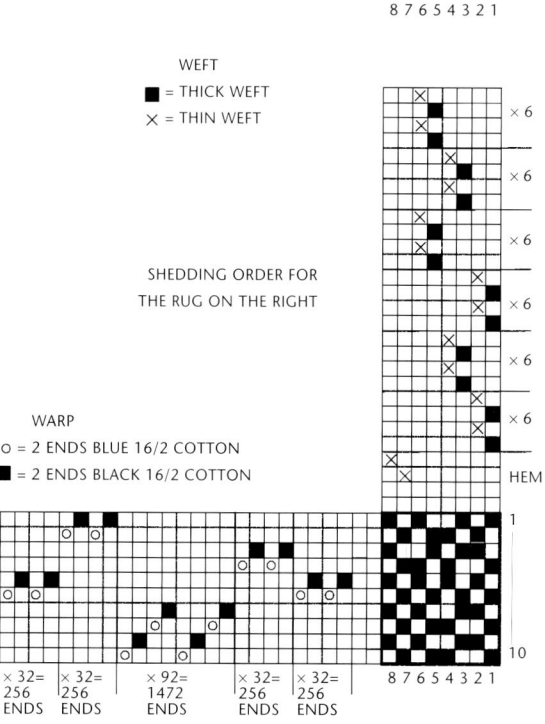

CRAMMED & SPACED REPP

Rosepath, diamond twill & dräll

The forerunners of the rugs in this section are entwined with childhood summers past. The richly patterned rosepath rugs are steeped in dreams and memories, pages 75-80.
The half dräll rug shows a white rag creating the pattern with various shades of rags in one and the same hue, page 82.
Diamond twill and dräll produce lovely patterns for rag rugs as well as rags with other wefts such as jute and Mattlin.

Top left: Rag rug in diamond twill, page 84.
Below left: Rag rug in half dräll, page 82.
Left: Rosepath III, page 80.

Rosepath I

DESIGN AND EXECUTION: ANNA SVENSTEDT

A rosepath rug with patterned stripes broken up with borders in blue or brown. A fine dark brown line of dashes defines the stripes. The entry for this rug is the same as for the Rosepath II and III rugs.

TECHNIQUE
Tabby with rosepath borders,
using 4 shafts and 6 pedals

WARP	12/6 dyed cotton rug warp yarn, grey col.nr. 1269, 2 850 m/kg, Borgs Vävgarner
WEFT	Washed single cotton rags, ca 2 cm wide
REED	30/10, 1–1
SETT	3 ends/cm
SELVAGE	2 ends to a heddle and dent twice on either side
WIDTH IN REED	71.6 cm
FINISHED WIDTH	69 cm
WEFT SETT	25 pattern picks and 25 tabby picks/10 cm
NR. OF ENDS	219
WARP REQUIRED	per meter: 80 g
WEFT REQUIRED	per meter: ca 1 kg

WEAVING
Use a stretcher and move it forward frequently. Weave a 5 cm hem in fine rags, then follow the weft sequence, see page 76.

FINISHING
Tie off 4 warp ends at a time in overhand knots. Trim leaving ca 1 cm of the warp. Turn the hems under twice and stitch down with rug warp yarn, passing between and around the warp ends.
(*cont. page 76*)

WEFT SEQUENCE

5 cm – hem, fine blue rags
6 cm – brown tabby accented by the dark brown dashes
7.5 cm – white ground with pale blue rosepath
6 cm – blue tabby accented by the dark brown dashes
7.5 cm – pale blue ground with blue rosepath
6 cm – brown tabby accented by the dark brown dashes
7.5 cm – white ground with grey rosepath
6 cm – blue tabby accented by the dark brown dashes
7.5 cm – pale blue ground with brown rosepath
6 cm – brown tabby accented by the dark brown dashes
7.5 cm white ground with pale blue rosepath
6 cm – blue tabby accented by the dark brown dashes
7.5 cm – grey ground with red rosepath
6 cm – brown tabby accented by the dark brown dashes
7.5 cm – pale blue ground with blue rosepath
6 cm – blue tabby accented by the dark brown dashes
7.5 cm – white ground with grey rosepath
6 cm – brown tabby accented by the dark brown dashes
7.5 cm – pale blue ground with brown rosepath
6 cm – blue tabby accented by the dark brown dashes
7.5 cm – white ground with pale blue rosepath
6 cm – brown tabby accented by the dark brown dashes
7.5 cm – grey ground with red rosepath
6 cm – blue tabby accented by the dark brown dashes
7.5 cm – pale blue ground with blue rosepath
6 cm – brown tabby accented by the dark brown dashes
7.5 cm – white ground with grey rosepath
6 cm – blue tabby accented by the dark brown dashes
7.5 cm – pale blue ground with brown rosepath
6 cm – brown tabby accented by the dark brown dashes
7.5 cm – white ground with pale blue rosepath
6 cm – blue tabby accented by the dark brown dashes
5 cm – hem, fine blue rags

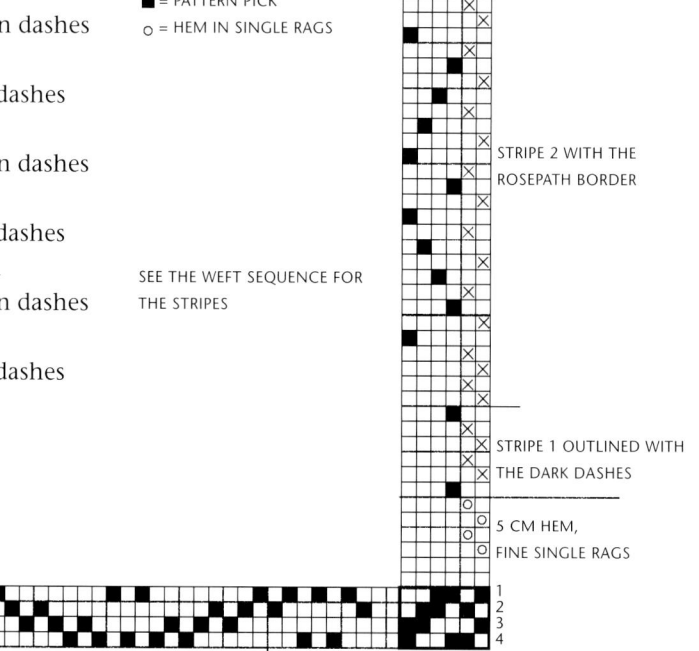

Rosepath II

DESIGN AND EXECUTION: ANNA SVENSTEDT

A classic. You can use up odds and ends in the stripes here. Sort them by color and chroma before starting to weave. The blue pattern woven borders with black and red stripes give the rug a genteel shaping. This is just how many of our peasant rugs were woven. The entry for this rug is the same as for the Rosepath I and III rugs.

TECHNIQUE
Tabby with rosepath borders,
using 4 shafts and 6 pedals

WARP	12/6 dyed cotton rug warp yarn, grey col.nr. 1269, 2850 m/kg, Borgs Vävgarner
WEFT	Washed single cotton rags, ca 2 cm wide
REED	30/10, 1–1
SETT	3 ends/cm
SELVAGE	2 ends to a heddle and dent twice on either side
WIDTH IN REED	71.6 cm
FINISHED WIDTH	69 cm
WEFT SETT	25 pattern picks and 25 tabby picks/10 cm
NR. OF ENDS	219
WARP REQUIRED	per meter: 80 g
WEFT REQUIRED	per meter: ca 1 kg

WEAVING
The tabby areas are woven in a number of different shades. This is where you can usefully rid yourself of odds and ends. Sort the balls of cut rags by color and chroma. Use them up in the order you put them into when sorting. If one rag type runs out, replace it with something similar.

FINISHING
Tie off 4 warp ends at a time in overhand knots. Trim leaving ca 1 cm of the warp. Turn the hems under twice and stitch down with rug warp yarn, passing between and around the warp ends. (*cont. page 78*)

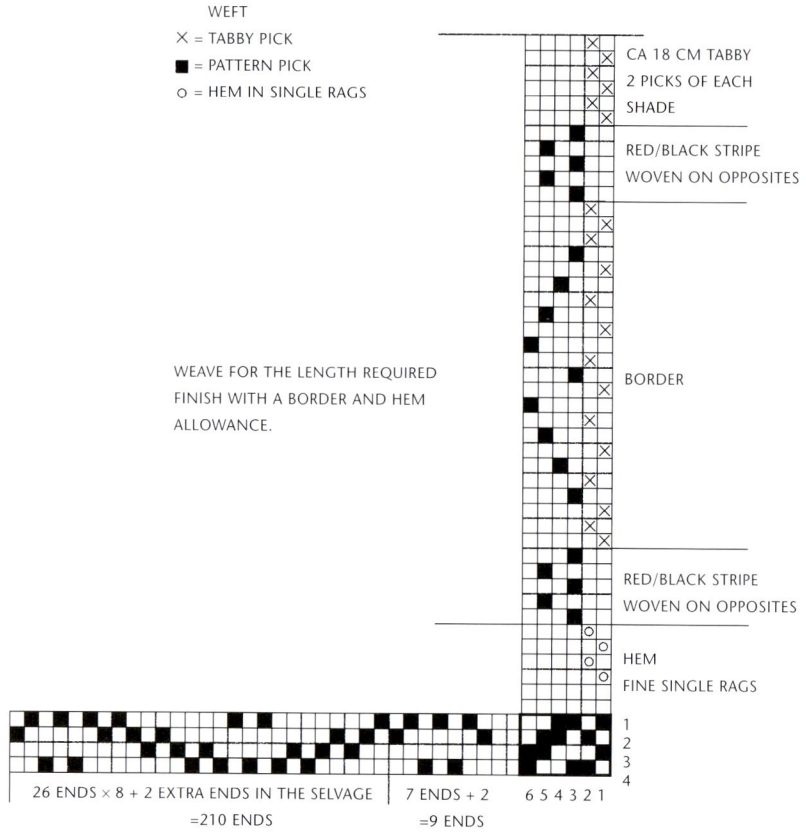

WEFT
X = TABBY PICK
■ = PATTERN PICK
o = HEM IN SINGLE RAGS

CA 18 CM TABBY
2 PICKS OF EACH SHADE

RED/BLACK STRIPE
WOVEN ON OPPOSITES

BORDER

WEAVE FOR THE LENGTH REQUIRED FINISH WITH A BORDER AND HEM ALLOWANCE.

RED/BLACK STRIPE
WOVEN ON OPPOSITES

HEM
FINE SINGLE RAGS

26 ENDS × 8 + 2 EXTRA ENDS IN THE SELVAGE = 210 ENDS

7 ENDS + 2 = 9 ENDS

6 5 4 3 2 1

78 ROSEPATH, DIAMOND TWILL & DRÄLL

Rosepath III

DESIGN AND EXECUTION: ANNA SVENSTEDT

This white and pale blue rosepath rug is indeed an ornament for the floor. The entry for this rug is the same as for the Rosepath I and II rugs.

TECHNIQUE
Tabby with rosepath, using 4 shafts and 6 pedals

WARP	12/6 dyed cotton rug warp yarn, grey col.nr. 1269, 2 850 m/kg, Borgs Vävgarner
WEFT	Washed single cotton rags, ca 2 cm wide (ground pale blue, pattern white)
REED	30/10, 1–1
SETT	3 ends/cm
SELVAGE	2 ends to a heddle and dent twice on either side
WIDTH IN REED	71.6 cm
FINISHED WIDTH	69 cm
WEFT SETT	25 pattern picks and 25 tabby picks/10 cm
NR. OF ENDS	219
WARP REQUIRED	per meter: 80 g
WEFT REQUIRED	per meter: ca 1.5 kg

WEAVING
Weave a 5 cm hem allowance in somewhat finer rags. Then weave the pattern for the length required, following the shedding order. Finish with a 5 cm hem again.

FINISHING
Tie off 4 warp ends at a time in overhand knots. Trim leaving ca 1 cm of the warp. Edge the rug with complementary fabric, machine stitching a French seam finish. You can also stitch the fabric edging to the rug, turn it over the rug edge to the back and secure with whipstitch.

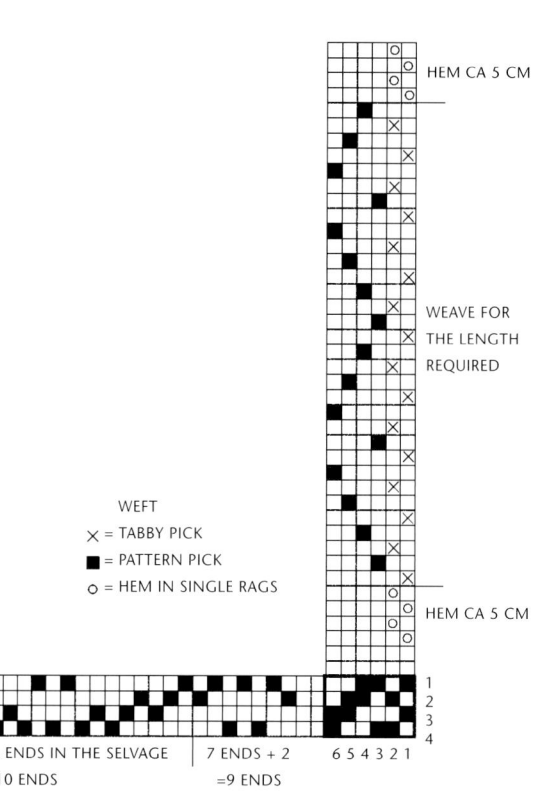

Half dräll rag rug

DESIGN AND EXECUTION: INGRID SKAGERSTRÖM

Undreamt-of potential for variation is what you get with half dräll. Using finer rags, you can weave checked or lengthways striped. One pick is in tabby, the next is a pattern pick.

TECHNIQUE
Half dräll, using 4 shafts and 4 pedals

WARP	12/6 unbleached cotton rug warp yarn, ca 2 800 m/kg, Blomqvist/Nordiska Textil-Garner
WEFT	Single rags ca 1.5 cm wide, checks woven with one white pick + diverse blues
REED	40/10, 1–1
SETT	4 ends/cm
SELVAGE	2 ends to a heddle and dent twice on either side
WIDTH IN REED	64.25 cm
FINISHED WIDTH	62 cm
WEFT SETT	1 check (for the rug illustrated) = 15 pattern picks + 14 tabby picks = 8 cm
NR. OF ENDS	261
WARP REQUIRED	per meter: 94 g unbleached 12/6 rug warp yarn
WEFT REQUIRED	per meter: ca 500 g white rags + 500 g in different shades of blue

WEAVING
Weave 8 picks of tabby in the rug warp yarn. Weave 6 cm tabby in finer rags for the turned hem. The hem allowance is woven plain colored or in narrow stripes. Weave checks 8 cm long, or checks and lengthways stripes as preferred.
NB! When changing block, no tabby is woven between the two blocks.

FINISHING
Tie off the warp ends in 2s and retain the 8 picks of rug warp yarn. Trim to ca 2 cm from the knots, tuck the warp ends under and make ca 3 cm turned hems. Use a thick needle and rug warp yarn, passing it around the warp ends of the rug. Pull on the thread as you stitch so the hem becomes as invisible as possible. Fasten off securely.

WEFT
X = WHITE RAG, TABBY
■ = BLUE RAG, PATTERN PICK
\ = HEM, RUG WARP YARN/FINER RAG, TABBY

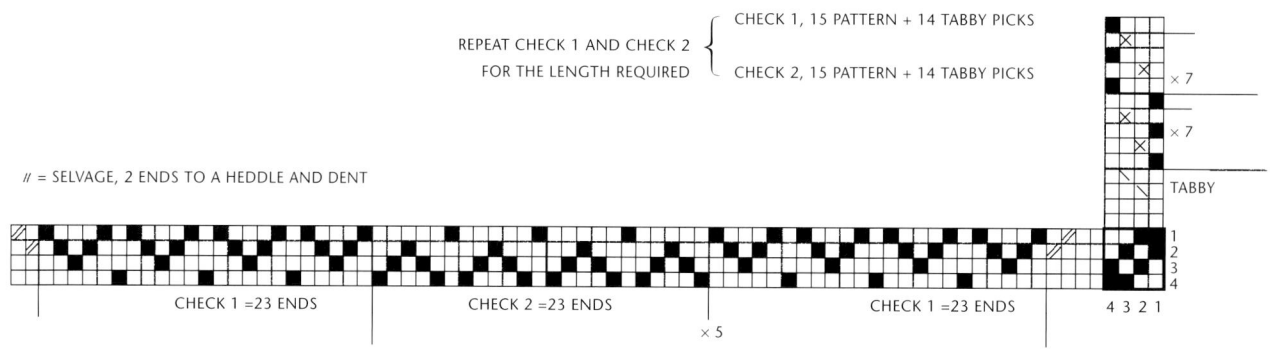

Diamond twill rag rug

DESIGN AND EXECUTION: STINA LARSSON

The basis of this rug was a little fragment of an 8th century cloth. A copy of that fabric was woven for Jämtland County Museum and the Museum of National Antiquities at the end of the 1970s. Stina Larsson converted the fine wool quality into a rug with a linen warp.

TECHNIQUE
Point reverse twill, using 4 shafts and 4 pedals

WARP	8/3 unbleached linen warp yarn, 1 700 m/kg, Bockens yarns, Holma-Helsinglands
WEFT	Cotton jersey rag strip, ca 4 cm wide
REED	30/10, 1–1
SETT	3 ends/cm
WIDTH IN REED	68 cm
FINISHED WIDTH	68 cm
WEFT SETT	5 picks/2 cm
NR. OF ENDS	204
WARP REQUIRED	per meter: 120 g
WEFT REQUIRED	per meter: 850 g cotton jersey rag strips

WARPING
Divide the number of ends in two and make two warp chains.

WEAVING
Make a heading for the rug of eight picks in the unbleached 8/3 linen warp yarn, arcing it well. The warp should be kept at a high tension while weaving and the weft laid in at an upwards angle. Never beat the weft down in an open shed. Use a stretcher, moving it forward frequently.

FINISHING
Cut the rug down and ply fringes as follows: Retain the headings. For every four warp ends from the rug, tie in another two doubled lengths of yarn. Then with four ends in each hand twist the bundles to the right. Pass the right bundle over the left until the fringe cord is the desired length, finishing with an overhand knot. Trim the fringe even a couple of centimeters from the knots.

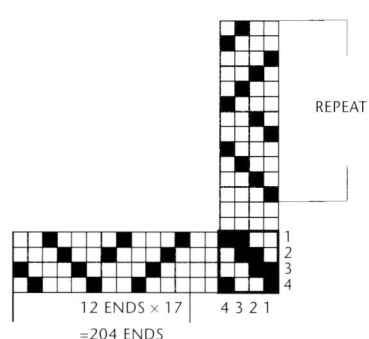

Crackle weave rug

REWORKING FROM THE ORIGINAL AND WEAVING: ALFHILD NICKLASSON AND MONICA MODIG RAUDEN

Crackle weave or Jämtlands dräll is a technique with a lot of potential. The original was woven with unbleached fishnet twine in the warp and unbleached and yellow handspun flax in the weft. The weft was substituted with Mattlin, available in loads of colors. If preferred the rug can also be woven in fine rags.

TECHNIQUE
Crackle weave, using 4 shafts and 6 pedals

WARP	12/6 dyed cotton rug warp yarn, blue col.nr. 34, 2 950 m/kg, Bockens yarns, Holma-Helsinglands
WEFT	4/6 Mattlin, blue col.nr. 1004, light blue col.nr. 134, 400 m/kg, Bockens yarns, Holma-Helsinglands or washed single cotton rags, ca 1 cm wide
REED	50/10, 1–1
SETT	5 ends/cm
WIDTH IN REED	83.8 cm
FINISHED WIDTH	82 cm
WEFT SETT	28 pattern picks and 28 tabby picks/10 cm
NR. OF ENDS	419
WARP REQUIRED	per meter: 142 g
WEFT REQUIRED	per meter: ca 600 g Mattlin in each shade or ca 1.4 kg cotton rags, 0.7 kg in each shade

WEAVING
Weave a tabby hem of 2–3 cm in the rug warp yarn. Use a stretcher and move it forward frequently. Follow the shedding order but do try out different block shedding orders to discover plenty of different patterns.

FINISHING
Tie off 4 warp ends at a time in overhand knots. Trim leaving ca 1 cm of the warp. Turn the hems twice, the width of the hem allowance woven in rug warp yarn, and stitch by hand. (*cont. page 88*)

BLOCK PATTERN ARRANGEMENT

RIGHT SELVAGE	7			
4 PATTERN REPEATS AT 98 ENDS		392		
PATTERN COMPLETION			13	
LEFT SELVAGE				7

=419 ENDS

The pattern is reversed on the other side.

BLOCK DRAFT
1 SQUARE = 4 ENDS/PICKS (STITCHING END AT THE BLOCK CHANGE)

The block draft shows the shedding order for the rug illustrated

WARP
■ = BLUE 12/6 COTTON RUG WARP YARN
╱ = STITCHING END, 12/6 COTTON RUG WARP YARN

WEFT
✕ = LIGHT BLUE MATTLIN
■ = DARK BLUE MATTLIN

98 ENDS × 4 =392 ENDS   EDGE   6 5 4 3 2 1

EDGE   COMPLETION

Rosepath and twill rug

DESIGN AND EXECUTION: STINA LARSSON

The inspiration for this rosepath and twill rug came from the old Härjedalen sheepskin coverlets. The combination of rags and linen stranded yarns in the weft produces a sturdy quality. An all-linen stranded yarn can be made quite simply with the help of a warping mill.

TECHNIQUE
Twill and rosepath, using 4 shafts and 4 pedals + 2 pedals for the headings

WARP	Boiled 8/4 linen warp yarn, col.nr. 0006, ca 1 200 m/kg, Bockens yarns, Holma-Helsinglands
WEFT	Three-fold weft consisting of 1 × 1.5 cm cotton rag, 1 × 3.5 cm jersey rag, linen stranded yarn from various linen yarns equivalent to 30 strands of 12 linen
REED	25/10, 1–1
SETT	2.5 ends/cm
SELVAGE	2 ends to a heddle and dent twice on either side
WIDTH IN REED	140.8 cm
FINISHED WIDTH	136 cm
WEFT SETT	11 three-fold picks/6 cm
NR. OF ENDS	356
WARP REQUIRED	per meter: 300 g
WEFT REQUIRED	per meter:
COTTON RAG STRIP:	700 g white/turquoise blend, 50 g turquoise green, 50 g dark turquoise green + 50 g white
JERSEY RAG:	1.1 kg white/turquoise blend, 85 g turquoise green, 85 g dark turquoise green, 85 g white
STRANDED LINENS:	400 g white

WARPING
Divide the number of ends and make several chains.

WEAVING
Weave a heading for the rug consisting of twelve picks unbleached 8/4 linen warp yarn. Arc it well. Follow the shedding order. The warp should be kept under a high tension while weaving and the weft laid in at an upwards angle. Never beat the picks down in an open shed. Use a stretcher and move it forward frequently. Wind the three-fold weft for the rug onto a stick-shuttle. Leave the stranded linen out of the narrow turquoise stripes of color to prevent too much of an increase in the weft sett.

FINISHING
Cut the rug off and ply the fringes as follows:
Retain eight picks of the heading. Taking four warp ends from the rug, tie in two extra ends double the length of the other ends. Holding four ends in each hand, twist to the right. Pass the right cord over the left until the fringe cord is the length desired, finishing with an overhand knot.
Trim the fringes even a couple of centimeters from the knots. (*cont. page 90*)

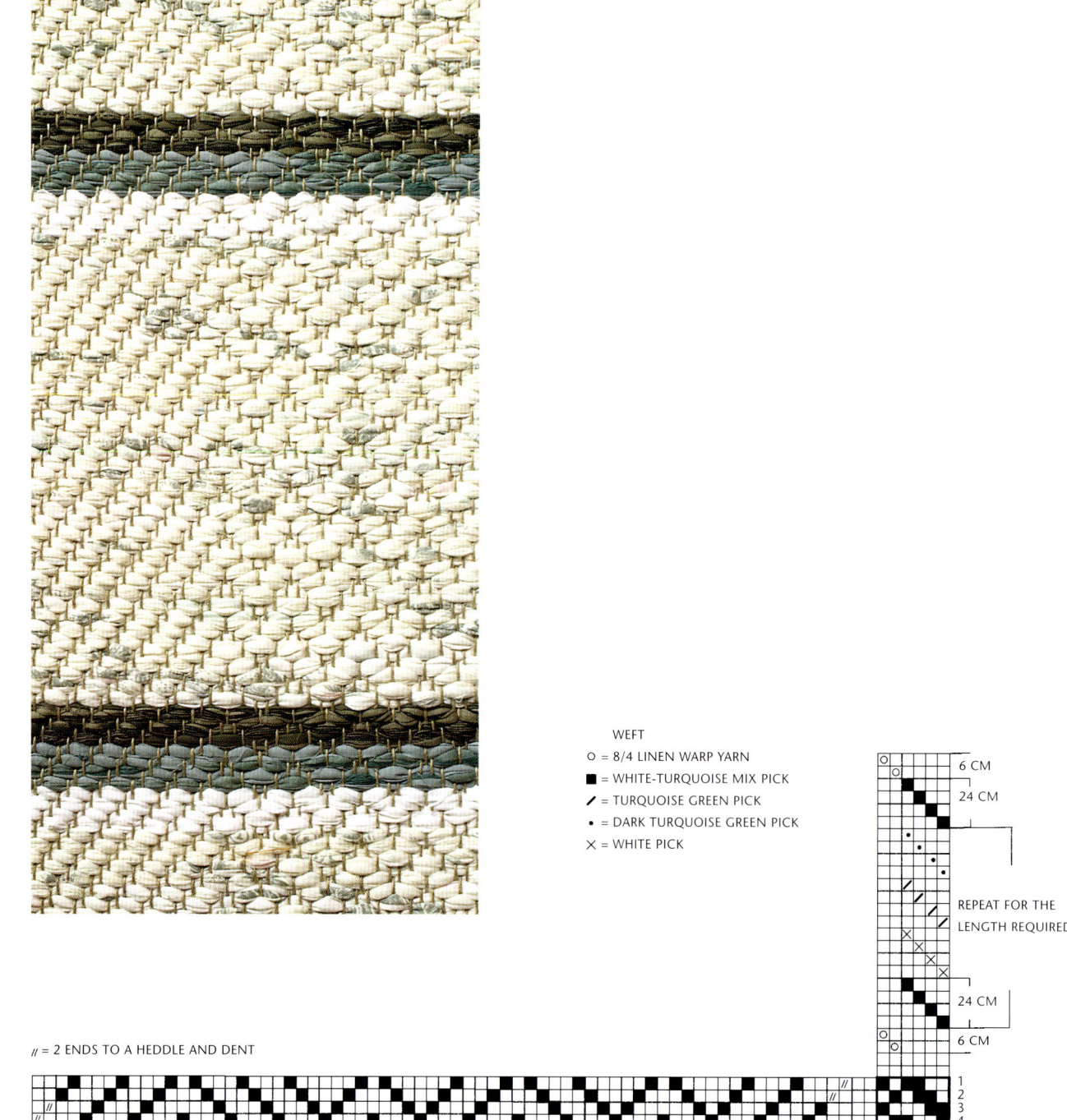

WEFT
○ = 8/4 LINEN WARP YARN
■ = WHITE-TURQUOISE MIX PICK
╱ = TURQUOISE GREEN PICK
• = DARK TURQUOISE GREEN PICK
✕ = WHITE PICK

// = 2 ENDS TO A HEDDLE AND DENT

Lapping waves on Vättern

WEAVE AND DESIGN: INGRID SKAGERSTRÖM

The model for this rug is a rosepath version to be found under the dining table in Ellen Keys' Strand on the Vättern lakeside. Perhaps the inspiration for the small wavy pattern came from the big lake. The rug is woven in three panels, two narrow and one wide centerpiece.

TECHNIQUE
Rosepath, using 4 shafts and 4 pedals

WARP	12/6 cotton rug warp yarn, olive green col.nr. 153, ca 2 950 m/kg, Bockens yarns, Holma-Helsinglands
WEFT	Single cotton rags 1.5 cm wide + 12/6 for the headings
REED	35/10, 1–1
SETT	3.5 ends/cm
SELVAGE	2 ends to a heddle and dent twice on either side
WIDTH IN REED	center panel, 79.7 cm; 2 side panels, 25.4 cm each
FINISHED WIDTH	center panel, ca 74 cm + side panels, ca 22.5 cm each = 119 cm
WEFT SETT	ca 44 picks/10 cm
NR. OF ENDS	center panel 283, side panels 2 × 91
WARP REQUIRED	per meter: ca 96 g for the center panel + ca 31 g/side panel
WEFT REQUIRED	per square meter: ca 1.6–1.8 kg cotton rags depending on how firm the beat and the type of rags used + rug warp yarn for the headings

WARPING
Make three warp chains. One for the center panel and one for each side panel.

WEAVING
Start with the center panel. Weave 8 picks for a heading in the rug warp yarn. Then weave 25 cm in the same rag wefts as will be used in the side panels. Weave the stripes, which in this rug are ca 11 cm long. Between each of the wide stripes weave a narrow stripe in a contrast color. Finish with 25 cm in the same rags as for the side panels and 8 picks of rug warp yarn. To keep a check on the length so it matches up with the side panels, run a non-elastic cotton tape alongside the weave. Measure with the warp under tension.

Then set up for the narrow side panel, or weave both side panels alongside each other. Use the cotton tape from the center panel weave as the measure. Leave all the pieces to relax and draw in for a couple of days before stitching together.

FINISHING
Retain two picks of the headings. Ply the fringes. For every 4 ends, tie in another two threads more than twice as long as the fringe will be. Each 4 ends with the extra 4 threads will become one 8-strand cord in the fringe. Finish the cord by wrapping one of the rug warp ends around the cord and making a half-hitch with it.

Then stitch the side pieces to the center panel. Use the warp yarn. To avoid the rug pulling out of shape, stitch into several different places to build up the seam.

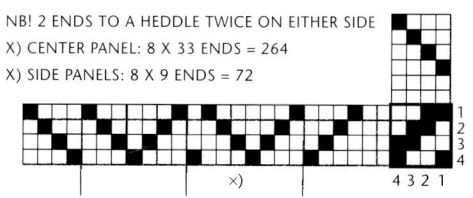

NB! 2 ENDS TO A HEDDLE TWICE ON EITHER SIDE
X) CENTER PANEL: 8 X 33 ENDS = 264
X) SIDE PANELS: 8 X 9 ENDS = 72

Watery reflections

DESIGN AND EXECUTION: EVA ARNESDOTTER SCHWYZER

Mattlin makes an excellent rug warp, giving the rugs a good weight and a beautiful luster. The dräll structure allows this warp to show and come into its own. The weft used here is sisal, but jute, paper yarn or rags all work well.

TECHNIQUE
Dräll, using 8 shafts and 8 pedals

WARP	4/6 Mattlin, blue col.nr. 134, 400 m/kg, Bockens yarns, Holma-Helsinglands
WEFT	Hem: 8/5 linen warp yarn, blue col.nr. 1388, 1 000 m/kg, Bockens yarns, Holma-Helsinglands Rug: sisal, blue, 260 m/kg, Lin & Lärft
REED	30/10, 1–1
SETT	3 ends/cm
WIDTH IN REED	72 cm
FINISHED WIDTH	ca 70 cm
WEFT SETT	Hem: 4 picks/cm; Rug: 20 picks/10 cm
NR. OF ENDS	216
WARP REQUIRED	per meter: 540 g Mattlin
WEFT REQUIRED	per meter: ca 560 g sisal + ca 50 g 8/5 linen warp yarn for the hems

WEAVING
Weave a 7 cm hem allowance in the blue linen warp yarn. Follow the shedding order. Finish with the hem allowance again.

FINISHING
Zig-zag carefully with a sewing machine over both ends. Turn under twice and hem down in close stitches. Press.

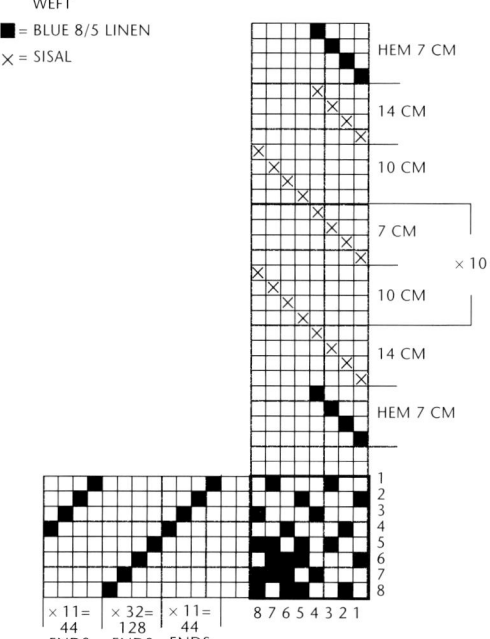

Twisted, thrown & patterned

Pattern and ground wefts combine to form the special character of these pattern woven rugs. Sometimes boundaries can disappear leaving the rags to wander free, as in Granite, one of the two "meet-and-part" rugs in this section.

In Puzzle pieces, a number of smaller rugs are woven up to be combined variously as changes of life dictate. These rugs are woven in double-faced weave, or two-block tied double weave as it is also known, and are reversible.

Top left: Meet and part, page 98.
Below left: Robust sisal rug in dice weave, page 100.
Left: Criss-cross inlaid tabby rug, page 107.

Meet and part

DESIGN AND EXECUTION: MARIE ROLANDER

A brilliant technique, where two different colored wefts form both the borders and the central field.

TECHNIQUE
Basketweave, tabby for the hem, using 4 shafts and 4 pedals

WARP	12/6 cotton rug warp yarn, grey col.nr. 1268, ca 2 850 m/kg, Borgs Vävgarner
WEFT	2 cm wide single cotton rags (NB strips should not be too wide)
REED	25/10, 1–1
SETT	2.5 ends/cm
SELVAGE	2 ends to a heddle and dent twice on either side
WIDTH IN REED	91.2 cm
FINISHED WIDTH	ca 87 cm
WEFT SETT	ca 20 picks/10 cm
NR. OF ENDS	232
WARP REQUIRED	per meter: ca 82 g
WEFT REQUIRED	per meter: ca 1.6 kg (0.8 kg in each shade) + rug warp yarn for the hems

WEAVING
Weave a tabby hem as follows: 1 cm rug warp yarn inserted in arcs, 6 cm rags, 4 picks rug warp yarn. Then weave the meet-and-part in basketweave. Insert the light and dark rag weft from either side. Twist the rags around each other the same way over/under the same warp ends 16 cm from the sides and return in the same shed. See the diagram. The meet-and-part places alternate, i.e. one on the left side, then one on the right. Fasten in the rags after weaving a good 16 cm and start again with the weft colors reversed. Weave for the length required and finish with the hem.

FINISHING
Tie off the warp ends in 2s, trim 1 cm down from the knots, turn and hem in close stitches with rug warp yarn.

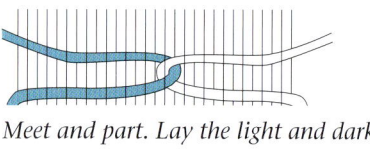

Meet and part. Lay the light and dark wefts in from either side.

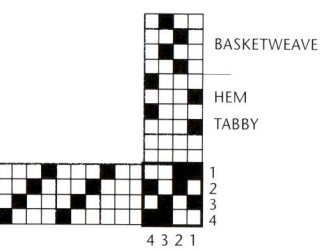

SELVAGE: 2 ENDS TO A HEDDLE AND DENT TWICE ON EITHER SIDE

Robust sisal rug in dice weave

DESIGN AND EXECUTION: MARIE ROLANDER

This sisal rug in dice weave is woven with dyed sisal yarn on a cotton rug warp. The design is easy to vary and you can use one or more shades of sisal.

TECHNIQUE
Dice weave (overshot), using 4 shafts and 4 pedals

WARP	12/6 cotton rug warp yarn, black col.nr. 1267, ca 2 850 m/kg, Borgs Vävgarner
WEFT	Tabby ground: 8/5 linen rug warp, black col.nr. 522, 1 000 m/kg, Borgs Vävgarner Pattern: 2 strands dyed sisal, ca 190 m/kg
REED	30/10, 2 ends to a heddle – 2 ends in every other dent
SETT	3 ends/cm
SELVAGE	2 adjacent dents double-sleyed on either side
WIDTH IN REED	85.3 cm
FINISHED WIDTH	83 cm
WEFT SETT	72 linen rug warp picks and 36 sisal picks/10 cm
NR. OF ENDS	258
WARP REQUIRED	per meter: 95 g
WEFT REQUIRED	per meter of rug: 650 g linen rug warp yarn, 1.7 kg sisal = 325 m, comprising 200 g blue, 1.5 kg grey

WEAVING
Weave a 4 cm hem in the linen rug warp yarn, making arcs of each pick. (Include a contrast yarn in a pick after weaving 1 cm to help stitch the hem straight later.)

FINISHING
Tie the ends off in twos in reef knots. Trim the warp a centimeter from the edge, turn under and hem in the cotton rug warp yarn. Remove the contrast yarn.

DYEING THE SISAL
Natural sisal is available in spools at builders' merchants, supermarkets or stationery wholesalers. Make big skeins of the yarn, for example round a warping mill, and tie off.

Dye with reactive or vat dyes for plant fiber.

Sometimes the yarn needs to be simmered before dyeing in order to absorb the dye.

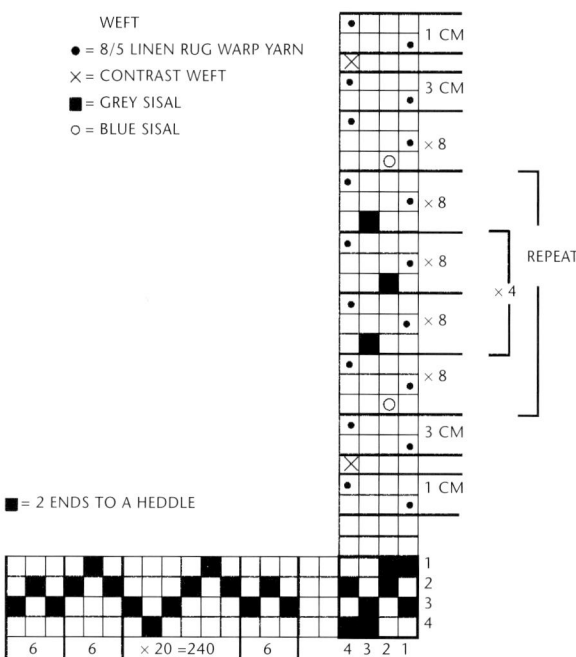

On the floor, over the table, up the wall

DESIGN AND EXECUTION: EVA NILSSON

A close weave narrow rug with a coppery ground and flaxen blue pattern weft. It works equally well as a long floor rug, hung on a wall or even laid out on a table.

TECHNIQUE
Tabby with pattern floats,
using 4 shafts and 3 pedals

WARP	12/6 cotton rug warp, brown col.nr. 1266, blue col.nr. 1265, 2 850 m/kg, Borgs Vävgarner
WEFT	Ground: copper colored single cotton rags, 2 cm wide Pattern: single blue cotton rags, 3 cm wide + brown 12/6 rug warp yarn for the hems
REED	35/10, 1–1
SETT	3.5 ends/cm
SELVAGE	2 ends to a heddle and dent twice on either side
WIDTH IN REED	53 cm
FINISHED WIDTH	49 cm
WEFT SETT	5 stripes of pattern floats + 5 tabby picks/10 cm
NR. OF ENDS	195
WARP REQUIRED	per meter: 68 g, ca 34 g in each shade
WEFT REQUIRED	per meter: 680 g ground, 340 g pattern

WARPING
Warp up with 1 strand brown + 1 strand blue together. Enter the ends as they come in no special order.

WEAVING
Weave 2–3 cm in the brown rug warp yarn. Then follow the shedding order for the length required. The first ground pick is inserted from left to right.

FINISHING
Tie off 4 ends at a time in overhand knots.

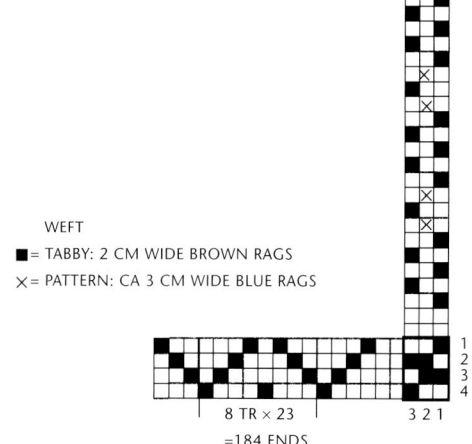

WEFT
■ = TABBY: 2 CM WIDE BROWN RAGS
X = PATTERN: CA 3 CM WIDE BLUE RAGS

8 TR × 23
=184 ENDS

Blue bows of sisal

DESIGN AND EXECUTION: GOTLAND COUNTY HANDCRAFT ASSOCIATION

Sisal is a rewarding material to weave with. Here, the tabby ground is in natural sisal and the weft floats in dyed sisal. For dyeing, see under the Robust sisal rug on page 100.

TECHNIQUE
Tabby with pattern floats,
using 4 shafts and 4 pedals

WARP	12/9 unbleached cotton rug warp yarn, 1 860 m/kg, Blomqvist/Nordiska Textil-Garner
WEFT	Sisal, undyed and dyed blue, ca 190 m/kg
REED	30/10, 1–1
SETT	3 ends/cm
WIDTH IN REED	81 cm
FINISHED WIDTH	81 cm
WEFT SETT	33 tabby picks/10 cm
NR. OF ENDS	243
WARP REQUIRED	per meter: 131 g
WEFT REQUIRED	per meter: ca 1 kg undyed + 300 g dyed sisal

WEAVING
Weave 12 picks of undyed sisal. Then weave the pattern as shown in the shedding order. Finish with 12 picks of undyed sisal.

FINISHING
Tie off 4 ends at a time in granny knots.

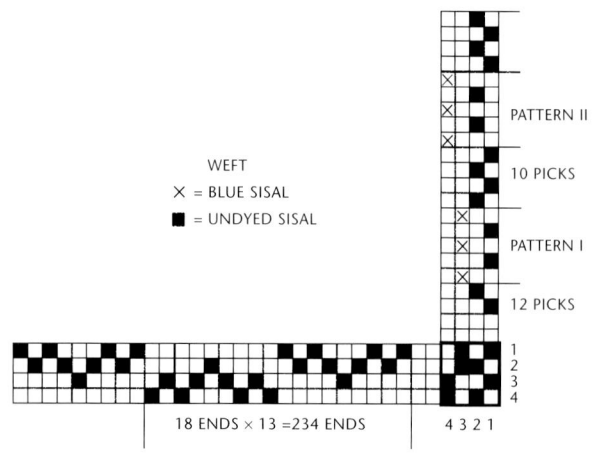

Criss-cross inlaid tabby rug

DESIGN AND EXECUTION: INGRID SKAGERSTRÖM

This is an ingenious way of inlaying a criss-cross pattern on a straight tabby. Linen rags in the weft on a bleached and blue linen warp produce a fine luster.

TECHNIQUE
Tabby with inlay

WARP	8/2 half-bleached linen, 2 420 m/kg
	16/2 dyed linen, blue col.nr. 296, 5 520 m/kg, Borgs Vävgarner
WEFT	Ground: cut white linen rags, ca 2 cm wide
	Inlay: cut linen rags dyed blue, ca 2 cm wide
	Hem: cut white linen rags, ca 1 cm wide
REED	40/10, half-bleached linen, 1–1; 16/2 dyed linen, 3–3
SETT	Half-bleached linen = 4 ends/cm; dyed linen = 12 ends/cm
SELVAGE	2 ends to a heddle and dent twice on either side
WIDTH IN REED	96.5 cm
FINISHED WIDTH	92 cm
WEFT SETT	20–21 picks/10 cm
NR. OF ENDS	428
WARP REQUIRED	per meter: 150 g half-bleached linen, 12 g dyed 16/2 linen
WEFT REQUIRED	per meter: ca 1 kg white linen rags for the ground, ca 50 g blue linen rags for the stripes and inlay + 8/2 linen for the inside hem

WEAVING
Follow the weft sequence on page 108. The inlay rag strips are secured on the reverse into a blue rag pick. The inlay passes over 2 picks then under 4 warp ends, see the diagram. Pay attention to the weft sett. The crosses can be placed wherever you want in the grid pattern.

FINISHING
Turn in the edges woven in linen yarn and under again. Hem down in strong linen, passing it in and out of the warp ends. Tug on the thread so the hem looks almost the same from either side. *(cont. page 108)*

WEFT SEQUENCE FOR THE HEM

1 cm – half-bleached 8/2 linen warp yarn

◄— fold line

10 picks – 1 cm wide white rags

◄— fold line

1 pick – 2 cm wide blue rag
2 picks – 2 cm wide white rags } ×3

1 pick – 2 cm wide blue rag ◄— first inlay

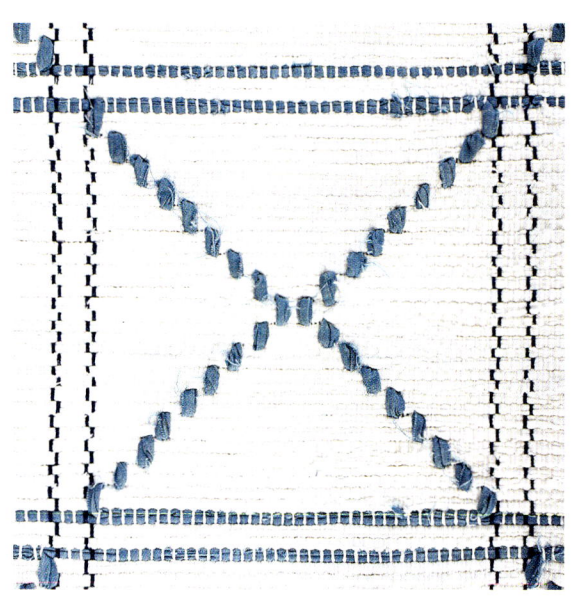

WARP SEQUENCE

							ENDS	DENTS
HALF-BLEACHED 8/2 LINEN	6		68		4		68	6	368	366
BLUE 16/2 LINEN		6		6		6		6	60	20
			× 4				=428	=386

WEFT
✕ = HEM AS GIVEN IN THE WEFT SEQUENCE
■ = CUT RAGS

WARP
✛ = DYED 16/2 LINEN, 3 ENDS TO A HEDDLE AND DENT
■ = 8/2 LINEN WARP YARN, 1 END TO A HEDDLE

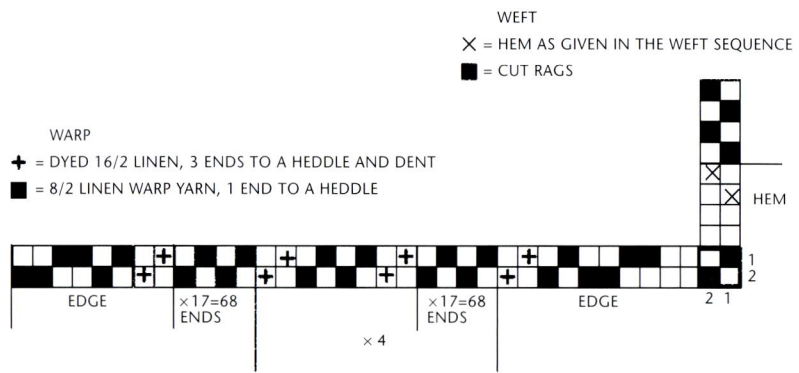

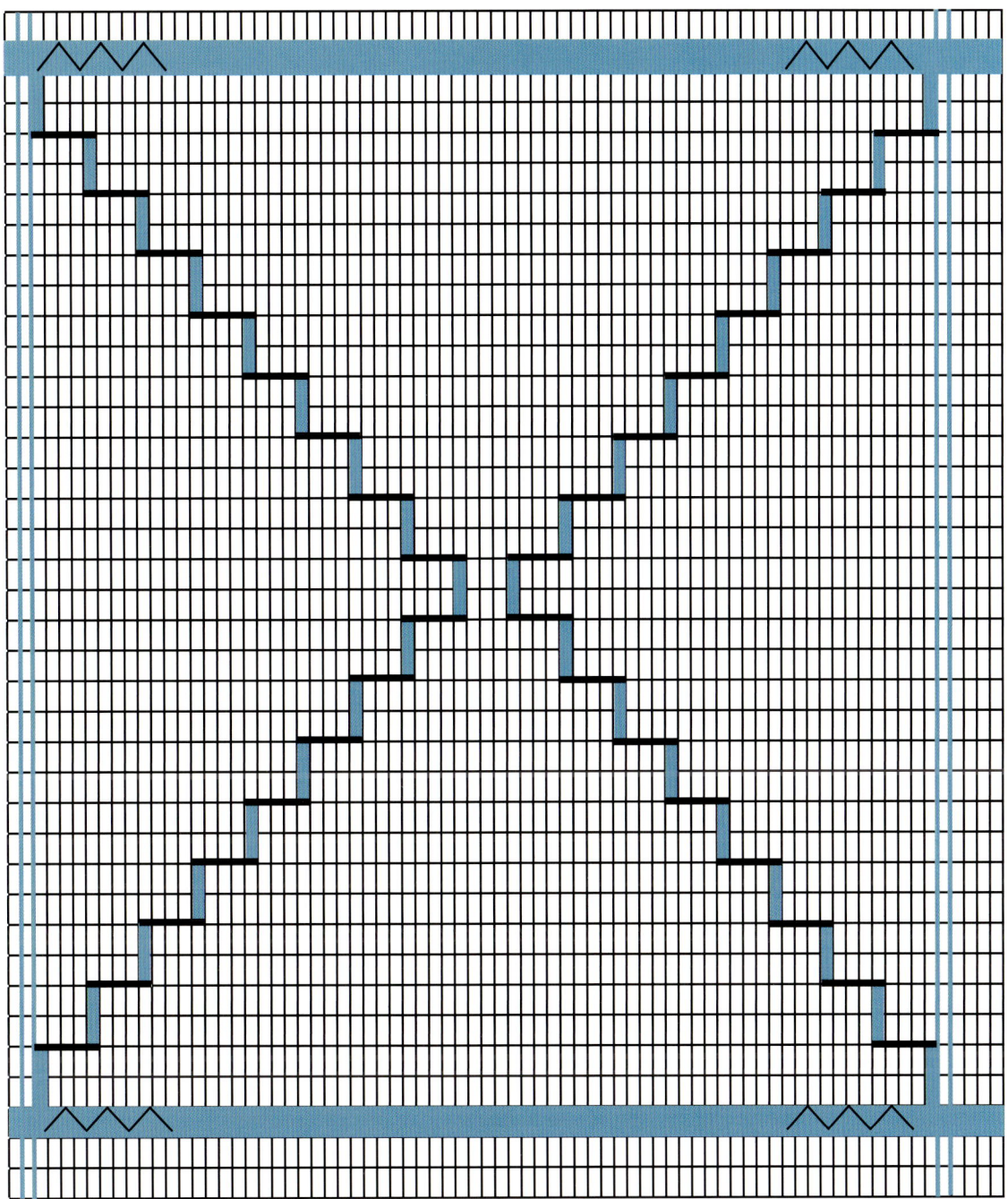

— = RAG PATTERN WEFT RUNS UNDER 4 ENDS ON THE REVERSE

| = RAG PATTERN WEFT RUNS OVER 2 PICKS ON THE FACE

∧∧∧ = RAG PATTERN WEFT FASTENED INTO A BLUE PICK AT THE BEGINNING AND END

ONE VERTICAL LINE = 1 WARP END
ONE HORIZONTAL SQUARE = 1 PICK
THE BLUE MARKS INDICATE THE INLAY ON THE FACE; BLACK MARKS SHOW WHERE THE INLAY RUNS ALONG THE REVERSE.

TWISTED THROWN & PATTERNED ✺ 109

Granite

DESIGN AND EXECUTION: CARINA RINDFELT

Weave this meet-and-part rug in greys of many kinds. Either weave it freehand or make a pattern design to follow.

TECHNIQUE
Tabby inlay in meet-and-part technique, using 4 shafts and 2 pedals

WARP	12/6 unbleached cotton rug warp yarn, ca 2 800 m/kg, Blomqvist/Nordiska Textil-Garner
WEFT	Machine dyed cotton rags, ca 2 cm wide
REED	30/10, 1–1
SETT	3 ends/cm
SELVAGE	2 ends to a heddle and dent twice on either side
WIDTH IN REED	74.5 cm
FINISHED WIDTH	73 cm
WEFT SETT	25 doubled rag picks/10 cm
NR. OF ENDS	228
WARP REQUIRED	per meter: 82 g
WEFT REQUIRED	per meter: ca 1 kg cotton rags

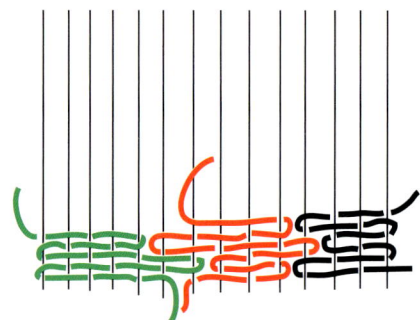

Lay the wefts in as follows. The weft on the very right is inserted from the selvage, while the others are laid in from either direction, as shown by the green and red wefts. The rug is built up with 2–4 wefts at a time of variegated rags.

DYEING
The fabrics for the rug were dyed black. A good way of obtaining different shades is to dye different types of fabric in the same dyebath. The grey shades appear when the dyebath is less concentrated.

WEAVING
Weave a 1 cm heading in the warp yarn.

Weave and add inlay or use small balls of each shade over the whole surface. The fields of color shift sideways after two picks, see the diagram. The wefts meet between two warp ends and turn without interlacing. The turns never happen on top of each other. Allow extra weft at the turns in the central part of the rug, otherwise small gaps can easily appear. If you want to compose a design beforehand, draw it out full-size on some transparent plastic. Fasten the pattern under the work as you weave.

FINISHING
Remove the heading, retaining 4 picks. Tie off 4 warp ends at a time in overhand knots. Trim the fringes down to ca 10 cm. For a more durable fringe, tie knots at the tips of all the warp ends.

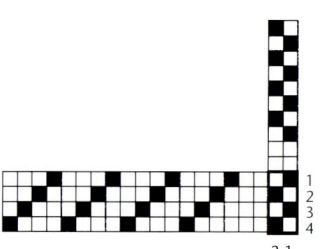

Puzzle pieces

DESIGN AND EXECUTION: MARIE ROLANDER

A collection of rugs with geometric designs. They can be pieced together into several small rugs or one big one, as circumstances change. Place the rugs slightly apart from each other with anti-slip matting underneath, or whip them together with longish stitches.

TECHNIQUE
2-block tied double weave; 4 shafts and 4 pedals for the plain, horizontal and vertical striped variations; 4 shafts and 8 pedals for the checked; + 2 tabby pedals

WARP	12/6 cotton rug warp yarn, beige col.nr. 44, ca 2 950 m/kg, Bockens yarns, Holma-Helsinglands
WEFT	Cotton rags, ca 2.5 cm wide + 12/6 rug warp yarn for the hems
REED	30/10, 1–1
SETT	3 ends/cm
SELVAGE	2 ends to a heddle and dent twice on either side
WIDTH IN REED	102.7 cm
FINISHED WIDTH	ca 95 cm
WEFT SETT	ca 4 picks/cm, 2 in each shade
NR. OF ENDS	312
WARP REQUIRED	per meter: ca 106 g
WEFT REQUIRED	per square meter: ca 2 kg cotton rags (1 kg in each shade) + 50 g rug warp yarn for the hems/rug

WEAVING
Weave a 3 cm tabby hem, arcing the rug warp yarn. It is worth inserting a contrast color yarn into the same shed as a regular pick after 7 mm, which will later help to keep the hem straight. (The contrast yarn is picked out once the hem is sewn.)

Weave as follows to make the right type of arc for the hem: throw the rug warp yarn in with one tabby pedal down, lay it in a big arc, change shed to the other tabby pedal before beating down.

Follow the shedding order for the checked, striped or plain variations. Measure the rugs with the warp under tension. For a square rug, weave ca 105 cm.

FINISHING
Tie off the warp ends in 2s and trim 1 cm from the knots. Turn the hems, with the help of an iron if you like, and hem with rug warp yarn in close stitches.

The pieces can be stitched together as a puzzle to suit the setting. Make big stitches so that it is easy to unpick them and make new rugs. The rugs can also be laid out alongside each other with little gaps between.

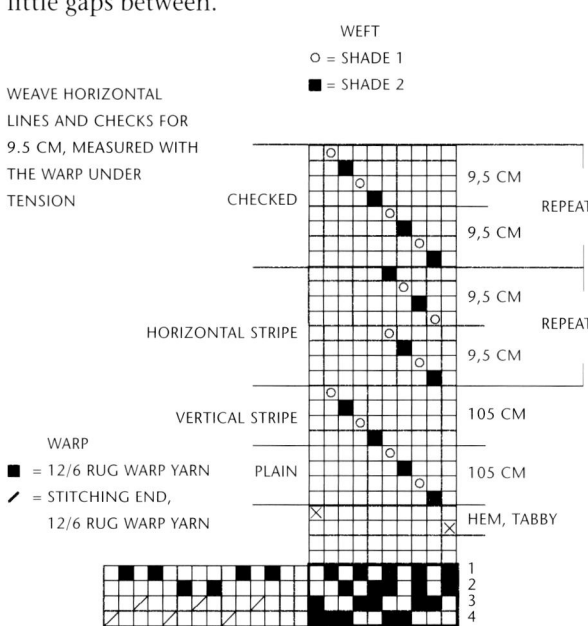

Five rugs on one warp

Leksands Hemslöjd created this series of variations with five very different rugs all woven on the same warp. A rag rug inspired by a simple stripe design kicks off.

The following rugs have stranded linen yarn, rushes or paper as weft. Stars shine white and bright on a midnight heaven of blue wool in the last variation.

Siljan

DESIGN: LENA HAGMAN   WEAVING: DAGMAR REINECK, LEKSANDS HEMSLÖJD

A simple striped rug in blue and white. With its classic design, it will be easy to place. Get inspiration from a ticking stripe or striped fabric, size it up and make a weave.

TECHNIQUE
Gooseye combination weave, using 4 shafts and 6 pedals

WARP	8/5 linen warp yarn, blue col.nr. 1388, 1 000 m/kg, Bockens yarns, Holma-Helsinglands
WEFT	Tabby ground weft: 8/5 linen warp yarn, as for the warp. Gooseye: blue and white linen rags, ca 2 cm wide, doubled
REED	25/10, 1–1
SETT	2.5 ends/cm
SELVAGE	2 ends to a heddle and dent twice on either side
WIDTH IN REED	87.6 cm
FINISHED DIMENSIONS	ca 85 cm × 2.5 m
WEFT SETT	14–15 linen warp yarn picks + 14–15 doubled linen rags/10 cm
NR. OF ENDS	223
WARP REQUIRED	per meter: ca 225 g
WEFT REQUIRED	per rug: ca 240 g linen warp yarn, 2.2 kg linen rags

WEAVING
Weave a 12 cm tabby hem in the linen warp yarn. Then alternate one pick linen rags with one pick linen warp yarn. See the shedding order. Use a stretcher and move it forward frequently. The stripes on your rug could be taken from a ticking stripe sequence or the stripes in part of a folk costume. Finish by weaving a 12 cm hem in the linen warp yarn.

FINISHING
Turn the hems twice and handstitch down to the reverse.

WEFT
O = DOUBLED LINEN RAGS, BLUE
■ = DOUBLED LINEN RAGS, WHITE
× = 8/5 LINEN WARP YARN

BLUE STRIPE

REPEAT. FINISH WITH 2 WHITE CHECKS + BORDER

× 5

WEAVE 2 BIG WHITE CHECKS

× 6

BORDER

× 2

TABBY

BORDER 14 ENDS | ×8 | ×8 | ×7 | ×7 | ×8 | ×8 | BORDER 14 ENDS   6 5 4 3 2 1

Stranded yarn linen rug

DESIGN: LENA HAGMAN   WEAVING: DAGMAR REINECK, LEKSANDS HEMSLÖJD

Make your own linen stranded yarn on a warping mill. Use finer and coarser yarns, bleached and unbleached. An excellent way of using up remnants. Perhaps do some experimenting with color blending. There are plenty of possibilities.

TECHNIQUE
Gooseye combination weave, using 4 shafts and 6 pedals

WARP	8/5 linen warp yarn, blue col.nr. 1388, 1 000 m/kg, Bockens yarns, Holma-Helsinglands
WEFT	Tabby ground weft: 8/5 linen warp yarn, as for the warp
Gooseye: linen stranded yarn comprising unbleached and bleached linen yarns and lintow
REED	25/10, 1–1
SETT	2.5 ends/cm
SELVAGE	2 ends to a heddle and dent twice on either side
WIDTH IN REED	87.6 cm
FINISHED DIMENSIONS	ca 85 cm × 2.5 m
WEFT SETT	18 linen warp yarn picks + 18 linen stranded yarn picks/10 cm
NR. OF ENDS	223
WARP REQUIRED	per meter: ca 225 g
WEFT REQUIRED	per rug: ca 245 g linen warp yarn, ca 2.8 kg linen stranded yarn

MAKE YOUR OWN STRANDED YARN
Arrange the yarns on a spool rack. Mix coarse and fine yarns, unbleached, half-bleached and bleached. Wind the stranded yarn around the warping mill and then into balls. For a good filler, use several thicker yarns in the weft mix.

WEAVING
Weave a 12 cm tabby hem in the linen warp yarn. Arc it well so the weft covers the warp. Then alternate one pick linen stranded yarn with one pick linen warp yarn. See the shedding order. Use a stretcher and move it forward frequently. Weave each check a little longer than it is wide. Take measurements with the warp relaxed. Finish by weaving a 12 cm hem in the linen warp yarn.

FINISHING
Turn the hems twice and handstitch down to the reverse.

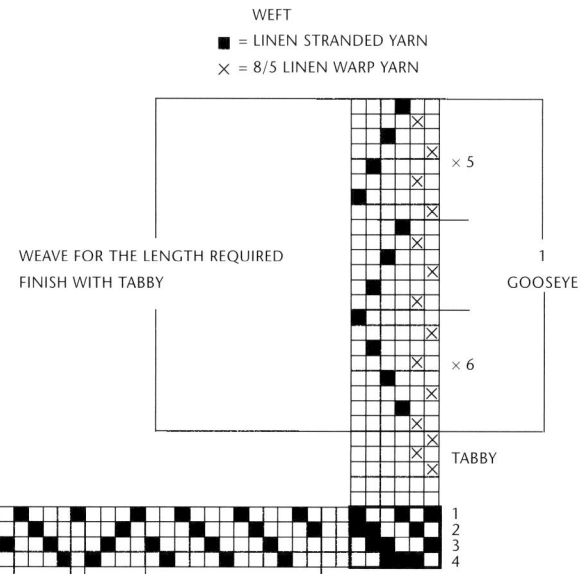

Sighing in the rushes

DESIGN: LENA HAGMAN   WEAVING: DAGMAR REINECK, LEKSANDS HEMSLÖJD

Rushes have long been used as rug weft. They are hardwearing and look good in a hall, a bathroom or out on the balcony.

TECHNIQUE
Gooseye combination weave, using 4 shafts and 6 pedals

WARP	8/5 linen warp yarn, blue col.nr. 1388, 1 000 m/kg, Bockens yarns, Holma-Helsinglands
WEFT	Tabby ground weft: 8/5 linen warp yarn, as for the warp Gooseye: rushes, Leksands Hemslöjd
REED	25/10, 1–1
SETT	2.5 ends/cm
SELVAGE	2 ends to a heddle and dent twice on either side
WIDTH IN REED	87.6 cm
FINISHED DIMENSIONS	ca 85 cm × 2.6 m
WEFT SETT	14–15 linen warp yarn picks + rushes/10 cm
NR. OF ENDS	223
WARP REQUIRED	per meter: ca 225 g
WEFT REQUIRED	per rug: ca 245 g linen warp yarn, 1.2 kg rushes

WEAVING
Weave a 12 cm hem in the linen warp yarn. Then alternate one pick of rushes with one pick linen warp yarn. See the shedding order. The thinner end with the feathery tip should be trimmed off. Piece the rushes by overlapping them. Dampen the rushes before weaving with them. Lay the rushes on some plastic and give them a shower while you are weaving. Rushes are soft and can be turned around the selvage ends. Finish by weaving a 12 cm hem in the linen warp yarn.

FINISHING
Turn the hems twice and handstitch down to the reverse.

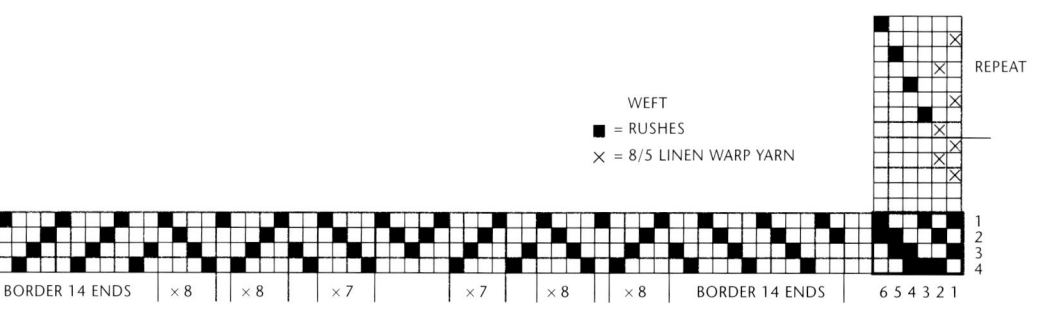

Relief

DESIGN: LENA HAGMAN   WEAVING: DAGMAR REINECK, LEKSANDS HEMSLÖJD

A thick twisted paper yarn produces a wonderful texture in a rug. Each pick of paper yarn is interspersed with several picks of the warp yarn. Gooseye makes for a lovely pattern effect.

TECHNIQUE
Gooseye combination weave, using 4 shafts and 6 pedals

WARP	8/5 linen warp yarn, blue col.nr. 1388, 1 000 m/kg, Bockens yarns, Holma-Helsinglands
WEFT	Tabby ground weft: 8/5 linen warp yarn, as for the warp. Gooseye: paper yarn Garland, green/blue blend col.nr. 026, 90 m/kg, Warp & Weft
REED	25/10, 1–1
SETT	2.5 ends/cm
SELVAGE	2 ends to a heddle and dent twice on either side
WIDTH IN REED	87.6 cm
FINISHED DIMENSIONS	ca 85 cm × 1.75 m
WEFT SETT	50 linen warp yarn picks + 10 paper yarn picks/10 cm
NR. OF ENDS	223
WARP REQUIRED	per meter: ca 225 g
WEFT REQUIRED	per rug: 995 g linen warp yarn, 1.6 kg paper yarn + 50 g linen warp yarn for the hems

WEAVING
Weave a 12 cm hem in the linen warp yarn. Then weave 5 tabby picks in the linen warp yarn between each paper yarn pick. See the shedding order. Finish by weaving a 12 cm hem in the linen warp yarn.

FINISHING
Turn the hems twice and hand-stitch down to the reverse.

WEFT
■ = PAPER YARN
X = 8/5 LINEN WARP YARN

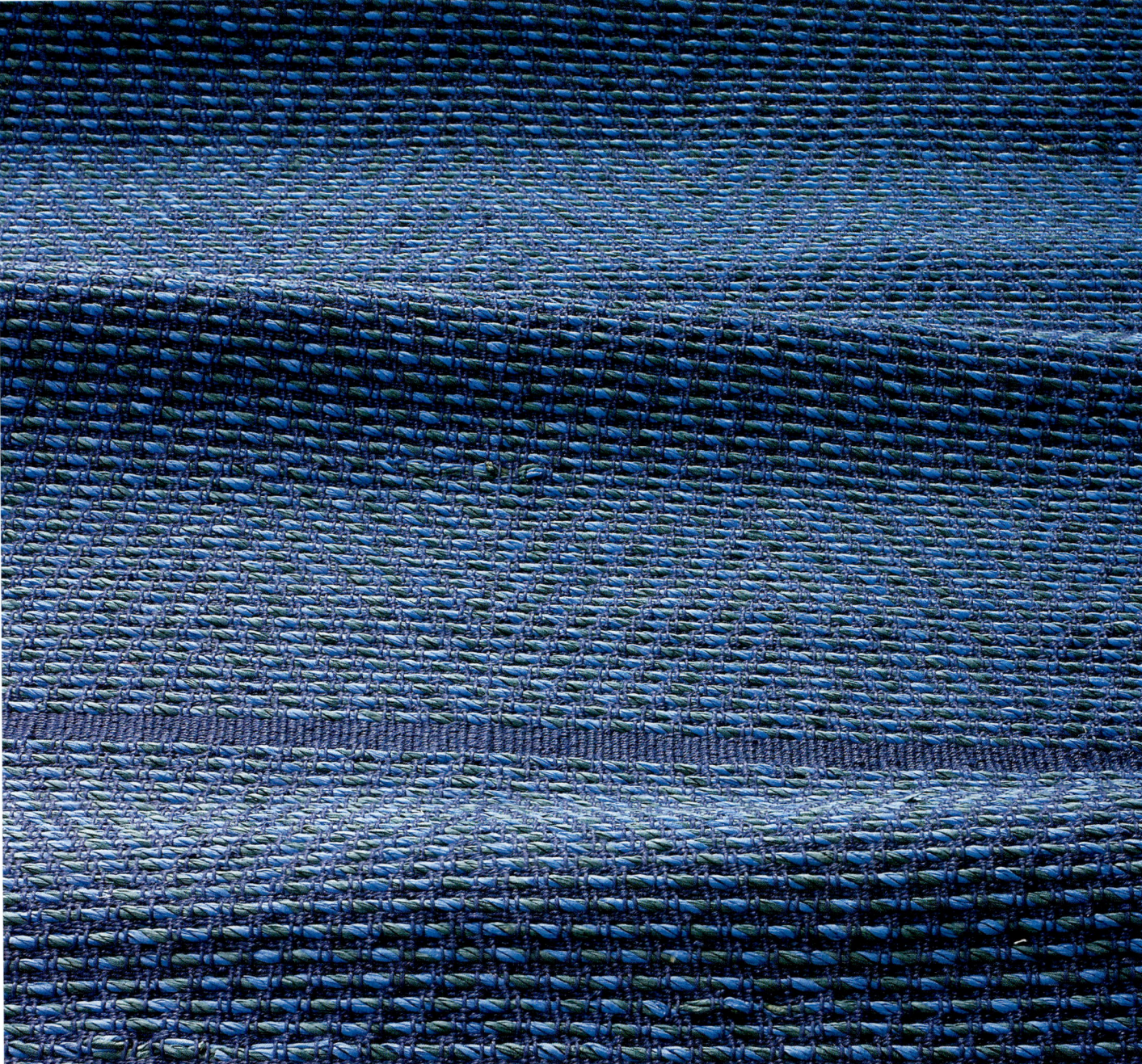

Twinkle twinkle lambskin stars

DESIGN: LENA HAGMAN   WEAVING: DAGMAR REINECK, LEKSANDS HEMSLÖJD

Dark blue yarn blended from wool and hair with small white leather strips of inlay create an exclusive rug. The patterning makes it that bit different. Stars shining bright in the sky at night.

TECHNIQUE
Gooseye combination weave, using 4 shafts and 6 pedals

WARP	8/5 linen warp yarn, blue col.nr. 1388, 1 000 m/kg, Bockens yarns, Holma-Helsinglands
WEFT	Tabby ground weft: 8/5 linen warp yarn, as for the warp Gooseye: Karvalanka (80 % wool, 20 % hair), triple stranded, blue col.nr. 7204, 500 m/kg, Warp & Weft Inlay for the stars: 14–15 mm wide × 5 cm long strips of fleece-less lambskin
REED	25/10, 1–1
SETT	2.5 ends/cm
SELVAGE	2 ends to a heddle and dent twice on either side
WIDTH IN REED	87.6 cm
FINISHED DIMENSIONS	ca 85 cm × 2.5 m
WEFT SETT	ca 20 wool picks + 20 linen warp yarn picks/10 cm
NR. OF ENDS	223
WARP REQUIRED	per meter: ca 225 g
WEFT REQUIRED	per rug: ca 340 g linen warp yarn, 3.2 kg wool blend yarn

WEAVING
Weave 2 cm in the linen warp yarn. Then alternate one pick three-stranded Karvalanka with one pick linen warp yarn. See the shedding order. Use a stretcher and move it forward frequently.

The stars are inlaid where the gooseye forms at the turn. The suede side of the leather strip lies against the rug. Lay the horizontal leather strip into the same shed as the wool yarn and poke the vertical lying strip in under the horizontal at the same time. Change shed and beat down. Finish by weaving 2 cm in the linen warp yarn.

FINISHING
Remove the headings, retaining 4 picks. Make a woven edge (*see the diagrams on page 126*).

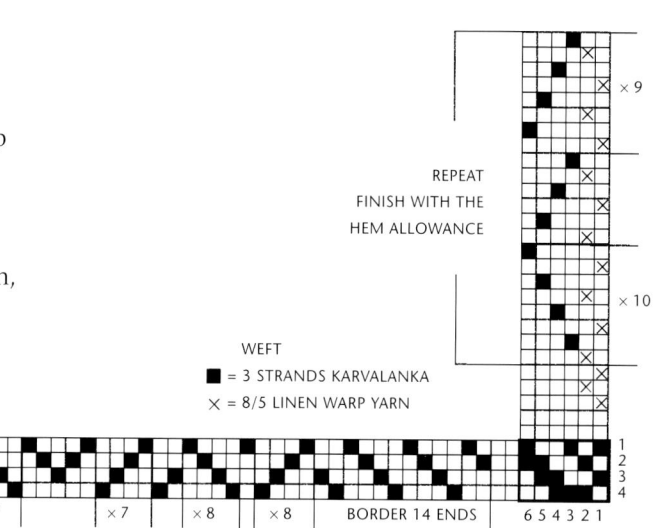

Woven edge finish

1. Retain 6 picks of the heading. Holding the warp ends, push the weft against the fell to firm up the edge. Tie simple knots with two warp ends (no double or overhand knots). To make the woven edge more substantial at the start, tie in an extra couple of ends (extra long) between the second and third knots. This pair of ends is woven in and out to the selvage ends three times. Each time the weft returns from the side it incorporates another pair of ends towards the middle. This first additional pair of ends continues to weave through the ends up to the space between the eleventh and twelfth knots.

2. Holding 12 pairs of ends taut in your left hand, make a shed for the weaving pair with the fingers of your right hand. Then pull the first pair of ends from the left (the outermost) to the right through the shed up towards the rug. Continue to work this way right across the rug.

3. Starting from the left again, thread each pair of ends with a rya or bodkin needle down through the space from the knot. Draw each pair of ends through the same way.

4. Starting from the left, the paired ends are now threaded into the next woven space and up through the heading into the ground weave of the rug. Pull the threads till the edge is firm. Trim the ends close to the rug weave and dab a spot of textile glue on the ends.

5. The final warp ends are finished in a plait.

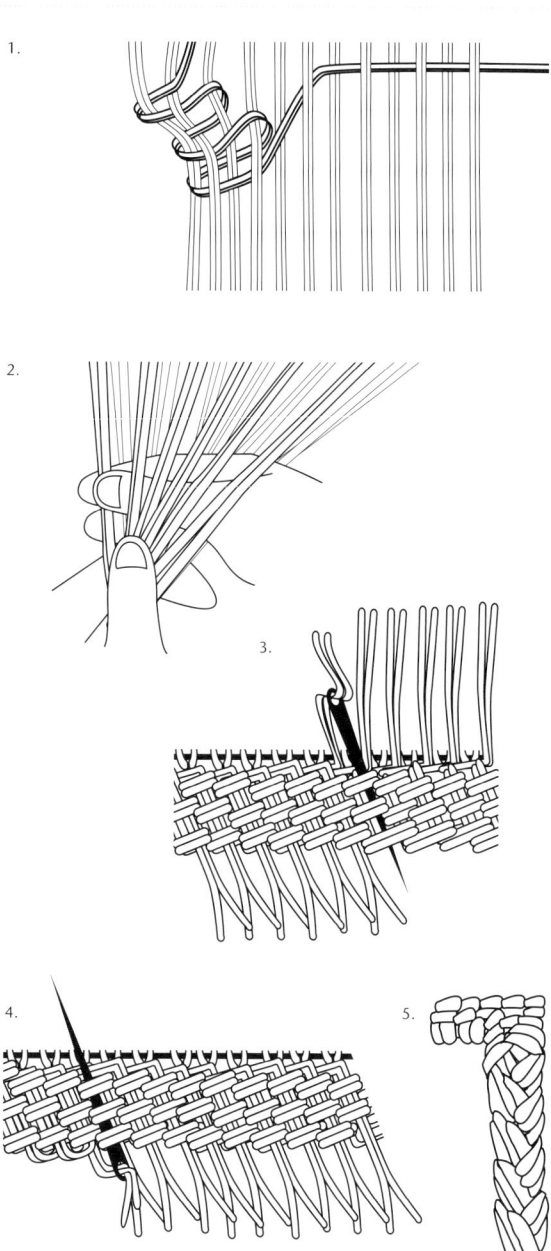

Inspiration

Deciding on the color scheme or stripe sequence for a rag rug is an exciting business. The rags to hand will partly lead the way but it is the actual sequence that forms the character. Look a little closer at Scandinavian peasant textiles: dress fabrics and ticking. There is an extraordinary wealth of pattern to discover.

Suppliers

Vävstuga Swedish Weaving and Folk Arts
16 Water Street
Shelburne Falls, MA 01370
(413) 625-8241
www.vavstuga.com
office@vavstuga.com
Swedish weaving supplies, looms, books, Swedish linens and cotton yarns. Classes also available.

Village Spinning & Weaving Shop
425 Alisal Road
Solvang CA 93463
(888) 686-1192 Toll Free
www.villagespinweave.com
villagespinweave@mac.com
We have warp yarns, weaving looms & all the tools.

The Mannings Handweaving School & Supply Center
1132 Green Ridge Rd
PO Box 687
East Berlin PA 17316
(800) 233-7166 orders only
www.the-mannings.com
office@the-mannings.com
Weaving materials, looms, accessories and classes.

Unicorn Books & Crafts, Inc.
1338 Ross Street
Petaluma, CA 94954
(800) 289-9276
www.unicornbooks.com
help@unicornbooks.com
Borgs weaving yarns, metal temples, stainless steel reeds, and Texsolv heddles.

The Weaving Works
4717 Brooklyn NE
Seattle, WA. 98105
(888) 524-1221
www.weavingworks.com
weavingworks@speakeasy.net
Looms, weaving supplies, warp and weft yarns, books, dyes and classes.

Woodland Woolworks
100 E Washington St
Carlton, OR 97111
(800) 547-3725
www.woolworks.com
info@woolworks.com
We carry looms, yarns, books, and equipment for the handweaver.

Rumpelstiltskin
1021 R St.
Sacramento, CA 95814
(916) 442-9225
www.yarnyarnyarn.com
rumpel@yarnyarnyarn.com
Looms, all kinds of warp & wefts, books, and offer weaving classes.

Glimakra Looms-USA
50 Hall Lane,
Clancy, MT 59634, USA
(406) 442 0354 / 1-866-890-7314
www.glimakraUSA.com
joanne@glimakraUSA.com
Glimakra weaving equipment, looms and accessories, cotton, linen and wool yarns from Sweden.

Louet North America
808 Commerce Park Drive
Ogdensburg, NY 13669
(613) 925-4502
www.louet.com
info@louet.com
Weaving equipment, yarns and more.

3425 Hands Road
Prescott, ON, Canada
(613) 925-4502
www.louet.com
info@louet.com

Canada (above and below)

Camilla Valley Farm Weavers' Supply
PO Box 341
Orangeville, Ontario
Canada L9W 2Z7
(519) 941-0736
www.CamillaValleyFarm.com
nmanners@camillavalleyfarm.com
Looms, Cotton and Linen Rug Warp, Books, DVDs, Temples and Weighted Beater Bars. North American subscriptions for VävMagasinet Scandinavian Weaving Magazine.